Excerpts from the Book

- Like many big decisions, buying a home is comprised of many small decisions rolled up into one big decision.

- About one in ten family's own a second home. That means most of us only get one. Choose wisely.

- Homeownership is the bedrock of building wealth.

- Rents are rising. One of the reasons for becoming a homeowner is to lock in a fixed cost of housing for you and your family.

- Homeownership is one of those areas in life requiring deliberate decision-making; there are very few accidental homeowners.

- Mortgage pay down is the one dependable wealth creator as a home-owner.

- What are the things you want close to your home that make a difference to daily life?

- Review crime statistics to gain as much information as possible about crime at and around the address of your potential purchase.

- No man, woman or potential homeowner is an island; you can't buy a home by edict or by command or wishful thinking. It takes a team.

- Home pricing is elastic and has much to do with consumer sentiment and the availability of mortgage financing.

- Buying a small apartment complex is a wonderful way to become a first-time homeowner because there are other people assisting in paying the mortgage.

- Some neighborhoods are so small that the demolition or construction of a single large building can dramatically change its demographic profile.

This publication contains the opinions and ideas of its author. It is intended to provide helpful and informative material on the subjects addressed in the publication. It is sold with the understanding that the author and publisher are not engaged in rendering accounting, financial or investment advice or any other kind of personal professional services in the book. The reader should consult their accountancy, legal and other competent professionals before adopting any of the suggestions in this book or drawing inferences from it.

The author and publisher specifically disclaim all responsibility for any liability, loss, or risk, personal or otherwise, which is incurred consequently, directly or indirectly, of the use and application of any of the contents of this book.

ISBN- 13: 978-0-9850027-7-0

12 STEPS TO HOME-OWNERSHIP

FOR FIRST-TIME HOMEOWNERS

Table of Contents

Introduction

Chapter 1: Step 1 Why buy a home?

The Big Picture 4

Rents Keep Rising 5

Affordability – How Much House Can I Afford? 6

A Place to Call Home 9

Changing Your Financial Life Forever 10

What the Federal Reserve Knows About Home-Ownership...... 12

Chapter 2: Step 2 Know Your Exit Strategy Before Buying

Your Home is Not Real Estate 17

Real Estate Investment Yield 17

Term of Residency 19

Term of Ownership 20

Moving time, Again 20

Chapter 3: Step 3Deciding on Property Type

Shiny & New versus Everything Else 25

Property Types 27

Chapter 4: Step 4 Demographics: A Changing Landscape

Demographics and the Direction of Change.............. 34

Demographic Data.. 36

Defining a Neighborhood of Interest 37

Defining Stats That Matter 38

Finding Stats That Matter.. 40

Chapter 5: Step 5 Geography: Choosing Where

A Simple Geo-Funnel 44

Choosing County, City and Drive-times 45

Safety: Quantitative versus Qualitative 46

Domestic Mobility 46

The Places in Your Life 47

Neighborhood Boundaries & Submarkets 48

Decisions that Bubble 48

Chapter 6: Step 6 Living the Life: Finding that Perfect Place

Decision Points 54

Pick Three 55

That Perfect Place 56

History and Reputation 57

Are You OK with That? 58

Chapter 7: Step 7 Choosing your Home Buying Team

Representation 67

Legal Counsel 68

Lenders 69

Chapter 8: Step 8 Home Loan Financing

Seeing Clearly 76

Preapproved vs Pre-qualified 78

Fixed versus Variable Rate Mortgages 82

A Note About Home Equity 83

Chapter 9: Step 9 House Hunting - The Search Process

Sticking to Your Guns.. 88

Flexibility Is Your Friend 90

Find That House! 91

Neighborhoods versus Zip Codes 92

Taking Notes.. 92

About FSBO'S, FIXER'S & REO'S 93

Passive Search 96

Active Search 96

Chapter 10: Step 10 Making the Offer

Natural Next Step 100

Waiting on Perfection.. 101

Acceptance 102

Chapter 11: Step 11 Home Inspection

The Home Inspectors List 106

Your (Home Inspection) List 107

Chapter 12: Step 12 Closing Day

Paperwork, paperwork.. 113

Almost home! 113

Create a Closing File 114

The Day After Closing 115

After Steps

You- the new homeowner. Wow! Things to do.................. 118

Conclusion...**121**

Are You Ready to Go Further? 122

Attention, Soon-To-Be Home-Owners! 123

Remodeling On A Budget – by John Wilhoit 131

Index 135

About the Author:

John Wilhoit has a Bachelor of Science in Business Management and a graduate degree in Urban Planning. In this book, John takes you through the ground-level nuts and bolts of home buying. John's approach is rooted in his 20+ years of experience in the real estate asset management profession and as a home-owner.

His perspective is further broadened by his experience in the public sector for federal and state agencies and in asset management for a publically-traded real estate investment trust. As an asset manager and owner–operator of apartments, condominiums and townhomes, John has developed his approach by administrating thousands of residences across the United States from pre-construction through development.

You will love John's book and the insight that he shares.

Join me at JohnWilhoit.com for updates, blogs, books, online courses and podcasts.

Other books by John Wilhoit

How To Read A Rent Roll: A Guide to Understanding Rental Income

Multifamily Insight Vol 1: How to Build Wealth Through Buying the Right Multifamily Assets in the Right Markets

Multifamily Insight Vol 2: How to Build Wealth Through Buying the Right Multifamily Assets in the Right Markets

Rent Roll Triangle: The Ultimate Rental Property Grading System

Look for John's book "Remodeling and Renovation on a Budget" coming out soon!

Preface:

What is the absolute hardest thing about buying a house? Getting started. The one over-arching objective I have for this book is to provide sound, practical, step-by-step guidance on buying your first home while avoiding as many pitfalls as possible. It's a book about getting started on your journey to home-ownership.

This book presumes your exclusive reason for purchasing a home is to live in the home. This book is for those considering homeownership and have a willingness to become educated about the process in advance so that when the opportunity comes their learning curve is short. This book is designed to prepare you for that moment in time when you can sign a contract for a home with confidence knowing that you've made a quality decision.

Homeownership is the bedrock of building wealth. There is no buying a second home, or third, without first buying the first one, right? Of course, there is far more to the process than just picking out a home with pretty colors and a nice door front. Answering the question of where you want to live creates a queasy feeling for many people; because we know where we "want" to live, then there is where we can afford to live. Balancing these two is part of the cognitive process of buying your first home.

This book is a do-it-yourself version to home buying providing tools and guidance for asking the right questions in advance of making the home buying decision. It is a guidebook to assist in your personal journey in the decision-making process based on your inputs and assisted by team members you select to work on your behalf to come up with the best choices for you and your family. Home buying is nothing that anyone should do on their own; building your own team is a necessary step in creating a successful outcome.

Acknowledgments:

Thanks to my lovely wife, Dr. Della Streaty-Wilhoit, for tolerating my intolerable commitment to completing this book. She reminds me often that what we carry around in our head is of little consequence unless shared with other people. This book exists only because of her loving prodding with the understanding that perhaps several thousand families could become homeowners based on following the steps outlined herein. If that becomes true, they should thank Della and not John. And to my niece, April, for requiring of me to outline "everything" so that her house-hunting could be concise yet comprehensive.

Introduction

The objective of this book is to draw a roadmap to the decision-making process for becoming a home-owner. I recently read an article about "the best places to become a first-time homeowner". This did not make sense to me, as people are uninterested in places "somewhere else" whereas they are VERY interested in purchasing a first home close to where they presently reside. This started me thinking about the cornerstone concepts to home-ownership and how to go about the process in sequence.

If you can purchase a home anywhere, what are some of the absolute realities a first-time homeowner should consider before buying. One of my primary objectives is saving you hundreds of hours and thousands of dollars in wasted time energy and effort in pursuit of homes that are outside of your sweet spot, personally, financially or geographically. I want you to stay focused on what works for you.

There are twelve primary steps to gaining home-ownership. Each of these steps along the way has Action Steps required to complete the journey: these are the "cobblestones" (smaller steps) beneath the steps- the bedrock for building your plan for getting through the entire process with grace and ease. The 12 Steps should be completed in sequence. The Action Steps provide some flexibility depending on your pace toward the goal of home-ownership. This book outlines three Action Steps in each chapter. The home study and online course expands this number.

In the 1800's most of America was open space with "homesteads" in the west and large landowners otherwise. On large working farms and ranches, housing was part of wages. In cities, there was "company housing". Rental housing ownership was concentrated also. Unlike voting, home ownership was a privilege- not a right.

Many readers will have family and friends that are homeowners. Certainly, some of your closest friends can provide some information about their own experiences. Yet, this is going to be your home. To use a simple example, who would you trust to go out and buy a car for you- sight unseen? Buying a home is one hundred times more personal.

This place will be your castle, your shelter, your home. So, while it is fine to seek input from family and friends the ultimate decision is yours- the one paying for the purchase. That said, in this book I point you towards real-life areas to contemplate, then accomplish. I want you to focus on your own pressure points and focus on the cognitive heavy lifting - the thinking that takes place before, during and after you begin the home search process.

My wife and I once purchased a home for our family in the rural Midwest. By rural I mean the city/town had a population of less than 50,000 people. The next biggest town was twenty-five miles away and had a population of 100,000. After that, it was another one hundred miles to a commercial airport. We set out with our wish list. Ranch home, one or more acres, close to schools and shopping. In our first day of looking, each property we viewed was five to eight miles out of town. We thought we were ready for rural…but not that rural!

Coming from a Washington DC suburb to the Midwest was shock enough. We had no interest in traveling five miles to the edge of town in hope of finding milk, eggs and butter. The response to our protest was this; "Oh honey, what your want is just not possible. All the land around here is taken up". Blink, blink. We had just flown over one thousand miles of America then drove one hundred miles to get to this location and per our sales person; there was not a single home on a single acre anywhere in the marketplace?

We decided on a colonial home on half an acre in town. The home had everything we wanted other than it was a two story. We were ok with that. We gave up on the ranch in exchange for getting everything else on our wish list. For us it was a fair trade.

The moral to this story is that without a pre-determined objective about the type of house you want, and where, someone else will decide this for you. Unfortunately, the classic story of failing to plan is planning to fail occurs repeatedly in home-buying.

When buying a home, as the dollar amount gets bigger, more and more people seem interested in the how, where and why you are buying a house. Please remember, that no matter the dollar amount, if you are buying a home with your very own money then your opinion is the only one that matters. The caveat being you will want the home to be of good quality and financially sustainable. Never wave inspections for expediency in pursuit of a home. Hire your own inspector that reports only to you. Inspect, review results, contemplate, proceed accordingly.

Chapter 1: Step 1

Why buy a home?

What makes the home buying decision so difficult? Because it is often both an emotional and financial decision. And, many people tend to tie their "self-worth" to the value range of the purchase (an unhealthy event to say the least). The home buying decision is hard because of fear; fear of making a mistake, fear of losing out on a better place (if only we had waited), fear of over-paying, fear of unforeseen market forces. Let me try to remove some of these fear factors.

For your entire life, you will require these three things: food, water and shelter.

For your entire life, you will require some place to live; why not own it? Yes, it is possible that mistakes are made, that prices are sideways, that your dream house sold before you could make an offer. All these things are possible. Yet one thing can remain as a positive constant by becoming a homeowner; at some point, you will own your home free and clear. This will never occur if you decide to remain a renter rather than become a homeowner.

The elephant in the room is this; many families are priced out of homeownership. As prices rise, homeownership affordability falls. There will always be some markets where it makes no sense to buy, considering rent vs own expenditure ratios, but not everywhere. In many markets, as rents rise and affordability dwindles, home-ownership is imperative as a tool of personal wealth building and as a defense against ever-rising rents.

The good news is that across the country there is a range of values for homeowners to choose from existing housing stock and new construction providing opportunity for families to become homeowners that never thought the American dream could become their reality.

In many instances being "priced out" means having to expand the search area. The trade-off is almost always longer commute times to job centers versus closer in neighborhoods. That trade-off, longer commute times to work to find more affordable home-buying options, is a staple of the home-buying process.

There are many good reasons to become a homeowner; to have a place to call home, a place to raise a family, with the potential for financial gain, peace of mind, in-door parking and gardening in your own back yard. What is YOUR reason for wanting to purchase a home? What makes this decision real for you?

Why become a homeowner? This seems like such an obvious and simplistic question but think about the ramifications. For the lifelong vagabond this is a huge psychological decision; it's an actual long-term commitment. For the large family moving from a two-bedroom condominium to a four-bedroom house with a yard it is a total lifestyle change; a change that requires adjustments personally and often, financially.

Try to segregate this thinking process about "why" from financial considerations. This initial decision (to buy or not to buy) is a standalone decision and separate and distinct from financial considerations. We all know people that can afford a home much bigger than the one they live in yet their home is "just right" for them. We all know people that could live in a "nicer" neighborhood than where they presently reside and this doesn't matter; they are staying put. These are two examples of people that have a housing choice and have made a long-term homeownership decision separate from financial considerations.

The Big Picture

Homeowners have something to pass on to their children. That's the big picture in a nutshell. Homeowners have a higher net worth than non-homeowners, much higher. Some home-owners are only passing on a large mortgage payment to the next generation along with the house, but not everyone.

Almost thirty percent (30%) of all homes in the United States are free and clear of any debt. This is the cornerstone of wealth building.

While it is nice to have stocks and bonds, oil wells and owned businesses, these investments are subject to much higher risk of loss than your home once owned. Companies fail, stocks can go up and down, bond values are subject to market flux and even real estate investments are not guaranteed to produce a yield. Yet homeownership, with appropriate financing, provides shelter and a place to live out your days a place that you have selected to enjoy with your family and friends.

Gaining homeownership with fixed rate financing or no debt also breaks the cycle of having to move and uproot your family at the whim of a property owner (read: landlord). Once a home-owner you are the property owner. And, to some degree, you get to pick your neighbors at least in terms of socio-economic status and educational attainment.

Having a fixed mortgage payment allows for better personal financial planning. While homeownership does require a reserve of cash for repairs and renovations the long-term affect is removing your family from market whims and rental price hikes that only seem to go up every year.

Rents Keep Rising

Rents are rising. One of the reasons for becoming a homeowner is to lock in a fixed cost of housing for you and your family. In markets big and small rents do rise. Granted they rise unevenly depending on the market but consider just the last ten years: even in times of recession and slow recovery, rents continue to rise at an average of three percent (3%) per year. Therefore, if you are paying $1,000 in rent today your rent will be $1,161 in five years and $1,359 in ten years.

In larger markets rents can and do increase five and ten percent each year. Using the same $1,000 in rent today that is increasing at five percent (5%) per year, in five years the monthly rental payment will be $1,283 and in ten years $1,647.

Following are reasons why rents will increase at a faster pace going forward.

- Limited new home construction and incremental population growth is a spark in the tinderbox waiting to explode. To maintain historic averages, in terms of the number of people per household, requires far more new homes in the pipeline.

- A limited supply of people in the construction trades continues to slow new development.

- A low interest rate environment is not sustainable. What is good for mortgage rates is bad for savers. There is no way no how that rates can remain low forever.

- Home ownership rates are decreasing creating an expanding renter pool. More people looking for rental-housing concurrent with limited new product points to higher rents.

- Home loan qualification is more difficult today. Higher underwriting standards decreases the number of families becoming homeowners therefore increasing the number of renters.

- Housing removed from service is restored at a slow rate; whether the cause is functional obsolescence, fire, flood or age. This is affecting available housing stock and represents another straw on top of the stack that makes for higher rents.

This creates a perfect storm for significant rental increases. Shelter, food, transportation and health-care are all mandatory pieces of our modern lifestyle. Shelter is the centerpiece. Being a homeowner with a fixed-rate mortgage allows you and your family to create a place called home that has fixed overhead costs going forward removing your family from rental increases year after year.

Affordability – How Much House Can I Afford?

While it's easy for many to look over the horizon and see great gains in real estate value based on macro-factors the bottom line is this; the home you can afford has a range of value between 1.50 and 4.0 times your annual income. Said another way: people purchase a home equal to 150% to 400% of their annual household income. This excludes a conversation about your initial down payment. Of course, a higher down payment amount could change the range of value provided above.

The home you purchase will likely range in value between 2.5 to 4.0 times your annual earned household income. Yes, there are many ratios that the new homeowner will need to fit into for purposes of obtaining mortgage financing. This range of value, of

2.50 to 4.0 times your annual family income is a guide to provide a starting point in thinking about price range.

Let's explore the atypical new home purchase using the values presented in the prior paragraph. A young couple fresh out of school and in their first jobs are presumed to have greater income as they progress along their career track. For the sake of example, let's say that their annual income is $50,000 dollars a year. At that level of income, a home purchase price of $75,000 is very affordable at 1.5 times annual income. Whereas, for the same couple, a home purchase of $200,000 is stretching and likely assumes no other financial obligations (such as car payments, student loans or credit cards).

For example, just because you can afford a home four times the amount of your current annual household income doesn't mean that's in your best financial interest in the long term. It is perfectly fine to go lower than 2.50 and, often, financially dangerous to go higher 4.0. The higher the ratio the greater the need for everything to go right, with respect to your household income, for an extended period of time.

Families change overtime; the family may decide that one parent should stay home with the children even if that means there is less household income. Conversely, perhaps one parent has the flexibility to work from home and therefore the family has decided to bring in a nanny to care for the children during the workday. This decision may require a larger home to accommodate the parent working from home.

These are examples where the size and price of a home is influenced by factors other than the cash down payment and financing options. I am asking you to stop and deeply consider your personal parameters about lifestyle and needs versus wants in a home, those that fit within your financial plan as determined by you and your financial advisors.

While this seems to be a rather generic range of value excluding other forms of income (such as passive income) the reality is that most first-time home buyers are not transferring assets from their portfolio to purchase their first home. Nor is there a magic wand that assist in finding the initial down payment. Down payment funds are most often procured from one of two sources; hard earned savings or family members.

Go to John Wilhoit.com for a free email course about 10 Ways to Find Your Down Payment.

Only for your own personal residence will I make this statement; price does not matter if the property is affordable considering your finances. Certainly, price is a factor in the buying decision and a quantitative aspect of the buying decision, however, when it comes to your personal residence the decision is a qualitative, subjective. Affordability at purchase, projected future income, decisions about lifestyle, location and personal comfort all fold into a discussion about price.

Buying a smaller house and freeing up dollars for savings is a worthy cause. So too is buying a larger home with the premise that it will fit your lifestyle for years to come without ever moving. Personal. Choice. Fold in the financial piece as a long-term lifestyle choice. Spending ten or fifteen percent more-or-less on the purchase will fade quickly in a short amount of time.

Paying real estate taxes annually are part of becoming a home-owner and impacts affordability. Always check the historic cost of real estate taxes for the specific address purchased. Here is why:

8

There is an amount of real estate taxes the current homeowner is paying annually. Depending on the municipality, this may or may not be the same number you, as the new homeowner, will pay. Regarding assessments for real estate taxes; some municipalities re-assess homes at sale, thereby increasing the taxes due from the subject property. Real estate taxes and tax rates vary significantly from state to state when a property transfers ownership.

A Place to Call Home

Making the decision to become a homeowner for some is a writ of passage to adulthood, or a stamp of societal approval that you are worthy to become part of the community. Walking through the doors of your first home brings excitement and fear: the excitement of new beginnings and the fear of how to pay for it all going forward.

Everyone wants a place to call home. The permanency that comes with home ownership really is a big deal. Not only do you now have a place to call your own, half the planet also knows where you live. Strangers will be calling your phone to hawk siding, roofing and windows. Boy Scouts and Girl Scouts will be at your door every year. Someone must cut the grass, move the snow and clear the weeds. Water heaters go out; pipes leak and door creak.

The balancing act of affording homeownership within your overall financial commitments is part of the processing to determine affordability for you and your family, figuring out how much house you can afford. Do you stretch with certain rosy presumption or remain conservative and buy a little less house? This decision will affect other parts of your life and lifestyle for years to come.

You put up with all of this for peace of mind, to own that little piece of heaven on earth to call yours; to have a place for celebrations and homecomings, a spot for your favorite chair and your very own kitchen painted in the exact color of your choosing to be changed whenever you feel like changing it. We hear it all the time; that home is where the heart is. Homeownership is one of those areas in life requiring deliberate decision-making; there are very few accidental homeowners.

Changing Your Financial Life Forever

With a brand-new mortgage in place on your new home, during the first few years much of the mortgage payment is interest on the loan with a sliver applied towards reducing the principal balance. This may seem unfair but it's the way of the world in mortgage financing.

So how do you ever get ahead paying 90% of your mortgage payment to interest expense? To a small degree, with the tax write off provided by the interest expense. Still, that is no reason to buy a home. Yes, it is a potential small benefit, but not the real reason to purchase a home. Here's the real reason…

Consider this: not one penny of rent ever pays anything towards a mortgage balance on your house.

Over time, more of the mortgage payment is applied towards principal until near the end of the loan term when the percentages are reversed with the majority of the payment applied to principal. Every month just a little (then eventually a lot) of your payment reduces your mortgage balance. Over time the house is yours free and clear of debt.

This is the incentive to stay put; owning a home free and clear of any mortgage. Increasing your mortgage payment amount, just a little, can shave years off the term. You can find plenty of mortgage calculators online to determine how much faster you can pay off the mortgage by increasing the payment by some amount. Even $100 a month has an impact.

Yes, we are skipping over the hay-day of people using homes like ATM machines getting cash out for vacations, cars and motorhomes. The next wave of re-financing paid for tuition, then weddings and more vacations. Mortgage balances never had a chance to go down with home prices soaring and people taking advantage of the opportunity to "cash out" as if the ride would never end. Well. The ride did end. Home prices tanked and millions of homes had mortgage balances higher than their value. But what if…

What if, instead of playing Russian Roulette with your home you just left it alone. Buy a home, get a loan and that's it- never refinance unless there is an opportunity to secure a lower, fixed, long-term interest rate. And when that occurs, reduce the loan term if possible, if the payment is the same or less than the original mortgage payment. What if that's all you ever did once purchasing a home. What would happen?

What would happen is that, eventually, you would own the home free and clear. No more mortgage payments. Yes, there is still taxes and insurance. But no mortgage payment forever more. It could happen to you. And it would change your financial life forever and perhaps that of your children and grand-children.

What the Federal Reserve Knows
About Home-Ownership

While there are no guarantees that homeownership will improve your financial wherewithal most people that own homes have a higher net worth than those that do not own homes.

The Federal Reserve is run by the Board of Governors of the Federal Reserve. The Federal Reserve Board of Governors is nominated by the President of the United States and confirmed by the Senate. Their role is to protect and preserve the economy of the country. Board members have a keen interest in the financial condition of consumers (citizens).

Once every three years the Federal Reserve completes a survey of consumers that includes information related to homeownership. The outputs of this survey range in value from one survey to the next, but the bottom line is this; homeowners are found to have a net worth of thirty to fifty times greater than non-homeowners. That's 30 to 50 times greater!!! Translated; a renter with a $5,000 net worth as compared to a homeowner net worth of $150,000 to $250,000.

Economist suggest that nearly seventy percent of the economy is driven by consumers; consumers that buy stuff. One of the things consumers buy is housing. Homeowners buy even more stuff to enhance the value of their new home. That homeowners have a net worth of thirty to fifty times that of non-homeowners.; that's the proof in the pudding.

Food for thought: Consider paying a small extra amount each month towards principal reduction on your mortgage. As little as $100 a month may reduce the term of your mortgage by one year or more. There are plenty of mortgage calculators on the web to make this calculation down to the penny. If you have a date certain goal for paying off your house you can back into the amount you would have to pay "extra' each month to hit that target date. It may be a smaller amount than you think so please check it out.

Action Steps

- Decide if you want to become a homeowner.
- Think about the financial ramifications of remaining a renter.
- Think about the cost of rent in five years versus the costs of homeownership.

Websites References:

- Zillow.com Home Buying Guide
- Forbes.com Buying a Home is Cheaper Than Renting
- Smart Asset.com Rent vs Buy

Chapter 2: Step 2
Know Your Exit Strategy Before Buying

By considering this question "what is your exit strategy" pre-purchase you are "backing into" how to buy your first home starting with the question; when do I sell? How many things do you buy with the intent to sell- even before you buy? Not many. And, this being your first home, here you are looking forward to settling in and I am asking you to consider the sell side- even before buying that first light bulb for your new home. If you could sell the home you are about to purchase, for twice what you paid... is it for sale?

I have a friend that says that every property he owns is for sale- even his personal residence. Now, there is not a "for sale" sign on the curb with blinking lights. But it is for sale. Every asset has an end game strategy to sell. The objective is to eventually sell the asset for more than you paid for it. The question is when and for how much? My objective here is to ask you to "pause and ponder". The market does not care whether you need to sell. Nevertheless, the cyclical nature of real estate markets provides uneven opportunities to sell.

Your Home is Not Real Estate

Your home, while looking like real estate, is not a real estate investment requiring a yield or income. Your home is the place where you live, love, entertain, laugh, cry, play loud music, rest. Your home cannot be relied on for income. While some will purchase small multi-unit properties as a homeowner, this is not the norm. And while you can rent out a bedroom for income unless this is a lifestyle it's probably only for a season. Nor should tax shelter be a major driver for purchasing a home as this is only true when there is debt and if current laws remain intact. Appreciation can occur but shouldn't be assumed as markets can be a roller coaster.

Real Estate Investment Yield

If your home were an investment it would generate all the forms of yield investment real estate is known to accomplish. Investment real estate provides four different forms of yield. They are:

- Income – as derived from rents or other ancillary income generated

- Tax shelter – provided by depreciation of the physical asset over time

- Appreciation – the increase in value over time

- Mortgage pay down – the small decrease in debt that occurs with each mortgage payment

Granted, home ownership can provide three of these four (and income too if you are renting rooms while retaining residency yourself).

Mortgage pay down is the one dependable wealth creator as a home owner.

Many consider it a forced savings plan. This is only true if there is debt, if there is a mortgage in place that adheres to historic norms; one that has principal and interest payments of a fixed nature. Using a variable rate mortgage can negate this if interest rates fluctuate significantly.

All this to say that treating your home as an "investment" can cause irrational thinking because owning a home is not exclusively a financial decision. The property could one day turn into an investment property, yes.

The premise of this book is that your exclusive reason for purchasing a home is to live in the home. The prior pages introduce homeownership as an existential wealth builder; creating financial benefits in the long-term and not as a trade play (buying and selling exclusively for profit potential). Real estate of any kind is a hard asset, an asset that has long timelines required to buy/sell/trade as compared to more liquid assets like stocks and bonds.

Financial benefits can occur when "moving up" from one home to another; potentially creating equity in house #1 that can be used to purchase house #2 and so on. Therein lies the longer-term benefit from homeownership; staying in place and ignoring changes in value based on short-term gains in equity and only selling when it is time to sell, personally.

I understand how hard this concept can be: "my house is worth $100,000 more than I paid for it three years ago!? Why would I not sell and capture this gain? Because then you must buy again if your intent is to remain a homeowner. Unless you are moving to a lower-priced neighborhood all the homes of interest have

18

also increased by this same amount. What have you gained? This excludes "fix and flip" or buying a foreclosure with significant repairs required. If you are in the market for another home "just like yours" then selling your home to purchase another just like it is nothing more than an exercise.

Term of Residency

Thinking about how long you want to live in a house is not easy and one decision that is glossed over in the giddiness of becoming a first-time homeowner. The best laid plans are often changed for reasons out of your control; a baby is born, a breadwinner becomes disabled, an elderly parent moves in unexpectedly. These are all events unplanned on move-in day. Most people do not like moving. The most common response provided to "how long will we live here" is; forever! Why? Stress. Because moving is hard. And time consuming. And expensive. It also requires of us to retrain our routine. So even if the move is a short distance with no change in job, schools, doctors or shopping patterns there is still an adjustment period required. Moves including distance, for job relocation or other good reasons, creates even more stress. Most people wish to avoid this.

Who is the house for long-term? Life changes, life events occur. Unfortunately, divorce rates remain very high. Our society has experienced economic events that impact the timing of when children leave the nest. The picture-perfect plan of changing little Mary's bedroom into an art studio maybe become significantly delayed based on events outside of your control. And while you cannot plan for every eventual change coming your way in life, please allow yourself some time for contemplation about livability for the people residing in the house long-term.

Term of Ownership

The act of buying a home doesn't make it a forgone conclusion that you will live there forever. People move for all kinds of reasons. Moving doesn't imply there is something wrong with the house. It may be a keeper as a rental.

Many people gain entrance to becoming real estate investors by moving from their first home and keeping said home as a rental. Great to do but please hire professional management for the new rental for the first year. Having a single-family home as a rental without professional management can be an absolute nightmare. Take that year and learn what property management entails before making the decision to take on management personally.

Moving time, Again

Homeowners move every five to seven years. Renters move every two years. This factor alone has personal and financial implications. When buying and selling stocks investors that churn their investments have higher transaction costs; they spend more on fees based on their buying and selling activity. This same principle holds true for homeowners versus renters that spend more actual dollars than homeowners in moving costs.

Let's take that dollar amount devoted to moving and multiply it over thirty years. The homeowner has moved four or five times (most likely to another purchased home). The renter has moved perhaps fifteen times with no potential to create any home equity all along the way.

You can see how this one factor can impact net worth. One family is moving practically every other year while another family is move every half decade or so.

Contemplating your exit before buying allows time for planning; it makes the buying decision "more real" and allows for creating a strategy that encompasses an end game- before the purchase.

Action Steps

- Recognize your home is not an investment asset intended to produce income.
- Consider the question: When do I sell?
- Think about term of residency and term of ownership.

Websites References:

- U.S. News - The Hidden Cost of Moving
- Money Crashers.com - Tips on Packing & Moving Cost
- Bigger Pockets.com - Real Estate Exit Strategies

Chapter 3: Step 3

Deciding on Property Type

When looking for homes it is necessary to narrow down the property type that fits you and your budget. Granted, it's fun to go to open houses that cost five times your budget, but the reality is you can afford only so much house. Price aside, what does your lifestyle lend itself to? Open spaces that may require longer commute times or city-center living that pinches the budget but provides that 24/7 city life that makes your motor run?

Truly Chasing Pavements

The objective of narrowing property type at the front end of the process is to keep you from beating the pavement to the ends of the earth. You should have an end goal in mind from the beginning that acknowledges your lifestyle as a cornerstone of the search process (see Chapter 6).

Yes, you will need to choose neighborhoods and get your financing in order, that's all part of the process. But before going there, are you a high-rise condo dweller or suburban office junkie needing your home close to the office because you (practically) live at the office eleven hours a day?

Do you care about architecture and "charm" or will any square box do that has decent parking and good signal strength for your gaming and streaming services? Is having natural light a priority or totally irrelevant? Does that mean a townhome is fine if an end unit with more windows or still, no, must be a single-family home? You must be honest with yourself. Selecting property type at the beginning will require addressing related lifestyle questions. Questions only you your family can answer.

Shiny & New versus Everything Else

In housing choice, new versus old is a big Y in the road. The new home building industry has well established buzz words to frame their product. New construction sales advertising includes words like: design-build, never-lived in and pick your colors. They all lead you towards the conclusion that you will be the first to have lived at that address.

In the world of new construction "old" is any home already sold. Why? Because home builders only intend to sell a house once. After that they have other new homes to sell. The best advice about new home builders is to pay close attention to their reputation.

There is just no getting around the fact that some home builders are better than others.

And, just like with the airlines, many have more than one division within the company; one may focus on "first class" another on "coach". Take the time to find out about the history of home builders in your marketplace and the level of quality and finishes made available in different subdivisions.

Retail stores are known to sell diamonds and diamond dust: it's important to know the difference. The same rule of thumb can be applied to home builders.

While the age of a home is a factor, quality of construction and upkeep are better determinants of long-term use and functionality. This is proven time and again in places like the Netherlands where there are homes approaching 500-years old that are still occupied to this day.

Aside from new construction, that leaves everything else. And everything else represents 95% of the housing stock. In my view, a home that is 3-5 years old, assuming it was not beat up, is still new because it will have had the benefit of the latest building technologies in use during its construction. This doesn't speak to finishes (cabinetry, high-grade flooring, etc.).

Building codes change all the time. The tussle here is between builders and municipalities about how current codes add to the durability and livability of a home. The parties will differ on perspective with the builders meeting current building codes adding to the cost of construction passed down to the consumer. This is not to say a five-year old home is better built that a ten or twenty-year old home, however, the major building systems are newer; roofs, windows, electrical, air-conditioning. And, it is likely the newer home has met the newest more stringent building codes.

As property ages, home-selling professionals have found new names for older homes, sayings like: mid-century, gentrified, charmed eloquence, and "in the historic district." Some homes are so beat up sellers give up on trying to describe the home itself and just focus selling the area or neighborhood, the geographic place. Examples, include Tribeca, SoHo, NoHo. These tag lines tell you nothing about actual homes, they just describe the neighborhood by name only.

Property Types

When most people think of homeownership they think of a single-family home, a place with four walls and a roof on a piece of land with a yard, maybe a garage. In most of the country this is the norm, but there are options that extend beyond the atypical single-family home. Let's look at homeownership by property type.

Single-Family home. Single-family homes will often represent the most expensive homeownership option. Why? Because single-family homes utilize the most physical resources in terms of land area, building supplies and on-going maintenance.

In its purest form, a single-family home has four exterior walls with the potential for windows on all four walls. A single-family home is detached from any other nearby homes. It is built on a plot of land segregated from appurtenant plots (appurtenant just means the land next to it on all sides).

There are now other forms of single-family that make the above definition "fuzzy". We have Planned Unit Developments (PUD), Age-restricted developments and other types of legal structures applied to single family. There are homes sold with the developer retaining a one-hundred year "land lease". These are some everyday examples of reasons to call on legal counsel for a review of documents to assure that the type of title being purchased is in alignment with your expectations.

Just about every piece of developable land sold has utility easements in place and mineral rights stripped by a prior owner. Developers advertise lot size that includes a front lot line beginning in the middle of the street. All these things may seem a little strange when you first hear about them but they are, frankly, common practice.

Townhome. A townhome is a dwelling that shares common walls with no more than two other dwellings where there are no other dwellings above or below the townhome. Townhomes are individually owned within a larger development. A townhome development will have assigned, or dedicated parking for each home. Some have attached garages or a grouping of garages that are individually owned. Townhomes will have monthly association fees, or common area fees. These vary widely from place to place.

Condominium. A condo is a living space, a dwelling, that can have similar dwellings above, below and on each side of one another. They can be individually owned, but they will always have other residences on two or more adjacent walls. Whereas a townhome is an individual home within a development where all the homes sit on the earth, condominiums are individual homes within a complex where only a small percentage of the complex sits on the earth. Excluding apartment properties that were converted to condo's, most are in buildings of three or more stories tall; therefore, a condo will have walls adjacent to two or more other condominiums.

There are many apartment properties that were converted to condominium use in recent years. In short, the biggest difference between a condominium built to be sold as condominiums and an apartment property converted to condominium use is fire code and amenities. Any apartment complex converted to condominium use must meet minimum fire code for condominium construction. With respect to amenities, a development originally built as a condominium will have a higher level of amenities than a converted apartment property; things like multiple pools, garage parking, fenced green space.

Condo fees and fee agreements vary widely; no two are the same. Some condominium associations collect for common area maintenance, real estate taxes and utilities. Others will collect exclusively for common area maintenance. Others for taxes and insurance and landscaping. Read read read...before you buy.

Duplex-Triplex-Fourplex. These multiple-dwelling properties can be considered for homeownership because, presently, homeownership financing is available for buildings that are 1-4 units in size. A building of five units or larger does not qualify for homeowner financing as 5+ units are considered commercial developments.

Buying a small apartment complex is a wonderful way to become a first-time homeowner because there are other people assisting in paying the mortgage. Using a duplex as an example, while your family resides in half the property a renter is living in and paying rent to you for the other side. Granted, there are drawbacks. Concurrently becoming a homeowner and landlord is buying a home and a job.

As a landlord, there are a multitude of rules and regulations to follow that would never come into play if you were to bypass this option. The fix is to interview professional property management companies and hire one prior to closing. They can onboard current and existing tenants while you focus on moving into your new home.

Mobile home. More than twenty million people live in mobile homes in the United States. In parts of the southeast some counties count most homeowners as residing in mobile homes. Do not discount this option as it starts the process of becoming a homeowner. The caveat with mobile homes is owning the land the home sits on. Without owning the land there is still rent to be paid even if your "home" is owned free and clear. So, while it is a step in the right direction the options presented above have a higher probability of building wealth over time: homeownership that includes owning all or part of the land underneath the structure.

Everything Else
There are "other" forms of homeownership. Does a Recreational Vehicle parked on a plot of land constitute homeownership? Is an address required to assume this is true? Everything else includes things such as Cooperatives (shared ownership), raw land, age restricted properties, boats, barns and caves (yes- caves). There is a legal structure for tenancy-for-life and life estates. The point is that getting mail in a box in front of a dwelling, while the norm, is not the only form of homeownership.

A Note About Homeowners Associations
Homeowner Associations encompass all types of developments today- not just condo's and co-op's. Some have only nominal responsibilities such as minor landscaping, others are fully staffed organizations responsible for landscaping and snow removal, architectural review and law enforcement. Fees can be $100 per year to $600 per month and higher. The association fee may cover costs for the community pool and a security patrol with an annual assessment that can change dramatically. Others include collective payments for taxes and insurances.

Any home that is within a homeowner's associations requires your full attention on the front end- before you buy- to understand the nature and level of services provided by the association. It is important enough that I ask you to seek out current and former home owners that have engaged with the association to get some real feedback on how the association works on behalf of the homeowners. Is it easy-peasy or a constant point of contention?

It's fine to dive in and become a board member. Otherwise, you have enough stress in life so avoid home-owner associations that require hours of your time each month about minutia. Life is too short to buy into hours of monthly administrative work when there are other options to consider without the noise or headache.

Action Steps

- What is your first choice in property type and why?
- Consider a second option for property type. Flexibility increases choice.
- Learn about the costs of maintenance for your choice of property type. Look closely at HOA expenses and management.

Website References:

- Trulia: 8-Questions That Predict What Types of Houses You'll Buy
- ProProfs.com What Kind of House Should You Live In?
- Trusted Choice.com - What Type of House Should I buy?

Chapter 4: Step 4
Demographics:
A Changing Landscape

The study of demography, or demographics, is the study of statistics about changes that occur within populations. At its most basic level, this study includes knowing about birth rates, death rates, the effect of disease. Pollsters survey "populations." Pharmaceutical companies test and run trials on very specific "populations" to study the impact of a new drug. For home buying purposes, the demographic focus is on social and economic variables that present dominant characteristics about the people that live in an area.

Demographics and the Direction of Change

As a future homeowner, getting to know your neighbors and understanding the demographics on a localized basis can assist in defining those places that match your intended lifestyle. Current trends, such as transportation districts and walkable cities, while providing real progress to the way we live in urban spaces, are also merely stepping stones in the evolution of how we live in urban areas and how we live together within communities.

There are two consistently overlooked areas in market demographics research as it pertains to home buying; the first is knowing what we have, the second is considering the direction of change.

A BIG part of what we have and/or what we are buying in a home is an area that represents an existing demographic profile. Ignoring this is like driving a car with your eyes closed. The remedy is simple; open your eyes and look around- and do the research. Federal, state and local municipalities spend millions of dollars collecting demographic information. Please take advantage of these resources.

A neighborhood can dramatically change in just a few years; from rusty and dusty to gleaming glass, from aging blue collar workers to young professionals. Some neighborhoods are so small that the demolition or construction of a single large building can dramatically change its demographic profile. The pendulum swings in extremes as some cities contract, then redevelop and revitalize. For example, recently more than twenty thousand people have move back into Chicago within two miles of city hall. The same is true in San Francisco. The opposite occurred in Detroit. These population swings have huge influences on local neighborhoods.

Review historic population, current population and the direction of change as a percentage of a baseline year. Census.gov is your best source for "snapshot" data of a place for an overview followed by local sources found at City Hall and county governmental offices. Getting granular will require more time and research. This is hard to do exclusively by search- you must go and see actual people in these places and ask questions about resources available to the public.

Something to pay attention to in your search is the ratio between owners and renters in neighborhoods. In Los Angeles, for example, approximately fifty percent of all households are renter households. That's not to say this is true in each neighborhood, of course. This is an important statistic to know when considering long-term ownership.

An underlying presumption of homeownership is that homeowners remain in one place for longer periods than do renters. Does a higher renter attribution pull at the fabric of community? No. Renters are usually younger and bring their energy to a place. On the other hand, if you have a young family, a neighborhood with a higher percentage of homeownership increases the probability that you kindergartener will graduate high school with at least a few kids they started out with at age five.

Demographic Data

Recognize that census data is broken down into smaller and smaller pieces beyond just county boundaries. Using public information, you can identify several data points that assist in determining the relative population levels and direction of change in population. Here are some definitions that overlay every neighborhood:

Block Group. Block Groups generally contain between 600 and 3,000 people, with an optimum size of 1,500 people. The census block group is the smallest unit of geography for which Census data are tabulated. Note that a single neighborhood may encompass more than one block group.

Census Tract. A census tract is a small geographic area. The primary purpose of census tracts is to provide a nationwide set of geographic units that have stable boundaries. Census tract numbers are unique within a county. A census tract will have from 1,500 to 8,000 persons with the optimal number being 4,000 persons.

Metropolitan Statistical Area (MSA). A metro area contains a core urban area of 50,000 or more population, and a micro area contains an urban core of at least 10,000 (but less than 50,000) population. Each metro or micro area consists of one or more counties and includes the counties containing the core urban area, as well as any adjacent counties that have a high degree of social and economic integration (as measured by commuting to work) with the urban core (from census.gov).

Defining a Neighborhood of Interest

People live "inside" their home and "outside" in the surrounding spaces and places that are nearby. The neighborhood is where we leave our abode and begin to interact with the outside world. Just on the other side of the front door interaction begins with the outside world.

What do you want in a neighborhood that just lights your fire? Do you desire a walkable place? Prefer a single coffee shop where "everybody" goes or choice? Is a commute to work of thirty minutes acceptable? What about an hour- each way? Is it important to have big box stores within an easy commute? What about family members that live close: do you want some spacing or prefer they are as close as possible to babysit the kids?

Are schools important or of no consequence? What about a library; important to you or gone with the dodo birds now that eBooks rule the earth? What about a church home? Do you attend three times a week or only on holidays? How about organized sports for kids and adults, or an adult learning center, or a senior's center?

Markets and shopping choice is assumed. Please, do not assume. Review what is available to you for basic food stuffs, restaurants and places that are on your short list of most-visited-favorite-places. Some people just love Dairy Queen and will pass up four other ice cream shops to go there. Personally, I like two grocery stores. I drive by many others to get to these. Where are these favorite places of yours in neighborhoods in under consideration?

Is your preference pure serenity or 24/7 action without ceasing? Do you own a car? Is street parking fine or does your "baby" require its very own house (otherwise known as a garage) with an alarm and sensor lighting? Do you want to interact with your neighbors or be left alone?

Answers to these questions will lead you to look at certain neighborhoods and eliminate others. Layering the following information on top of your answers will begin the process of defining the neighborhoods for your home search.

Defining Stats That Matter

The remedy to driving blind (demographically speaking) is to perform an analysis of the in-place population looking at population trends that includes the number of people, their household income, average family size and educational attainment, looking also, at the direction of change in each of these categories.

Population growth. Look at 'local' population growth. We all know of parts of our city that is a "ghost town". People move for all kinds of reasons. Find out if the areas of consideration for your purchase are increasing or decreasing in population and why.

Household income. Income at the household level for an area is a point of comparison to city, county and state levels. Is average family income higher or lower than for other parts of town?

Average family size. Smaller family size means there are a lot of single people in the area. Nothing wrong with that but it tells you to take a closer look as schools. If family size is shrinking in the area that may lead to school closures and school closures means that your kids could be attending a different school in the future than the one assumed.

Educational attainment. It is well documented that third-grade reading levels tell us much about adult achievement. There is a direct correlation between personal income and educational attainment. Over-stating the obvious, people with a college degree make more money than high school drop outs.

Three cities in the United States with some of the lowest high school graduations rates are; Detroit, Las Vegas and Miami. Does that mean these cities are unattractive markets for homeownership? The answer cannot be established based exclusively on local high school graduation rates. The reason being that a high percentage of people residing in these cities migrated there from somewhere else. Why? Jobs. People follow jobs.

Reading levels are important to understanding adult achievement, educational attainment and high school graduation rates. From a demographic perspective, the most interesting statistic is the educational attainment of current residents. People with higher education (college) and those with higher reading levels have higher incomes. People with higher income are more likely to become homeowners. Thus, there are higher homeownership rates in neighborhoods with higher educational attainment. Neighborhoods with high educational attainment are neighborhoods with high levels of home ownership. These two factors are joined at the hip.

Average Age. Just another point of reference. Are you looking at a neighborhood where most residents are over the age of sixty-five? If yes, what happens to the neighborhood in ten years? Big turnover to come, right? Will homes be swooped up by those interested in preservation and gentrification or landlords? What's the trend? Is average age high or low, increasing or decreasing? Do you like what you see or is there cause for concern given your lifestyle choices? Are you looking to make new friends to run with or people to befriend your parents when they are in town?

Race. Important to some people, not at all to others. My thinking is that diversity provides a richness to life that is absent when everyone looks and thinks exactly the same. Others would disagree. Living in a neighborhood without any form of diversity (cultural, regional, by color, religion, language) is like being married to yourself; you may like yourself just fine, but it must get a little boring talking to someone that agrees with you ALL the time.

Finding Stats That Matter

U.S. Census. There is Census.gov, American Fact Finder and State and County "Quick Facts" All of these are courtesy of the U.S. government.

State and Local government offices. Many governmental departments found at the Federal level are also in place at the state level. For example, every state has its own Department of Agriculture that is like USDA, but state-wide only. Same for Commerce and many others. Many of these departments create and use demographic information and make their data sets available to the public at no cost.

Bureau of Labor Statistics. BLS.gov provides a free mapping tool with a huge cache of data related to economics and demographics. This Federal government website has tables and on-screen data on inflation and pricing, employment, unemployment, pay and benefits, spending and time use, productivity and employment projections. And it is free to access…

Universities. The Departments of Social science, Economics and Agriculture use and produce data sets for research purposes. And not just four-year schools. There are many 2-year colleges providing local research in study areas that attract and acquire local demographic data sets. Many universities also have Extension that serves as a catalyst for the university to connect and provide services about state run programs in local communities.

Action Steps

- Go to Census.gov and review American Fact Finder for your city.
- Find local resources of demographic information.
- Ask questions and determine where people are moving and why.

Website References:

- U.S. Census.gov
- Neighborhood Scout.com
- American Fact Finder (Census.gov)

Chapter 5: Step 5
Geography:
Choosing Where

This chapter will require of you to think through the "where" part of your new home purchase.

Where do you want to live? I mean really. And who do you want to live "around"? Thomas L. Friedman of the NY Times discusses this often in his columns; how changes to neighborhoods impact the dynamics of what people think locally and globally.

This chapter outlines a road map on the journey to determining where. Use the following neighborhood characteristics as a flashlight into the corners of places. Look in all the corners you possibly can. It is ok to find some dirt and grime, everyplace has its dirt and grime.

A Simple Geo-Funnel

Every 'place' is in a neighborhood, that is in a city or county, that is in a state, commonwealth or providence, that is in a country. Reversing that order, as a potential homeowner you must choose: Country-State-County-City-Neighborhood-Street. Think of this as a 'geo-funnel".

Country-State-County-City-Neighborhood-Street

Please, please take the time to pre-determine the best locations for you and your family, first, without outside influences. Along the way, you may discover some hidden neighborhood gems that have everything you ever wanted. Then, expand the search and the number of people you are willing to listen to after creating the initial cut of locations.

Create your very own initial geo-funnel. Then, over time, add more neighborhoods that meet the same criteria. Granted, the list will eventually get small. But initially, the world is your marketplace to search until that time as you have selected that special place (or places) to consider growing roots.

Choosing County, City and Drive-times

For home purchasing purposes, you must choose a country and state. This sounds simple enough, yes? Then choose a county of residence for the purchase of your new home. This may sound like an over-simplification but consider that many people reside in tri-county areas where they live in one county and work in a different county. Now chose your city of residence, the place to become a homeowner. Here is where the work begins. For most people country-state-county is easy, even city can be a breeze. Now what?

Start with drive times or commute times; how far are you willing to live from your job? What is an acceptable commute? Consider miles and drive time as these can vary significantly from place to place. What if you were to change jobs? Does this impact your decision-making process? In larger cities commute times can include more than one mode of transportation; drive to train station, take train to city, for example. Or walk to metro or bus, exit at your stop and walk the remaining distance.

Let's start with a simple question: what country do you wish to live in? This question is simple for most people. Most people reside in the country of their birth. This is where you grow up becoming educated and learn socially acceptable behavior, morals, values, laws and government structure. This is where you make friends, have families and grow old.

Safety: Quantitative versus Qualitative

When it comes to the selection of a neighborhood most will say their number one priority is the safety of their family and possessions. Safety has two components; quantitative and qualitative. Quantitative are those things we can measure like the number of break-ins and crimes against people and property. Quantitative is not subjective. The fact is that some neighborhoods have more crime than others. Qualitative attempts to answer the question "how does that make you feel?". What are your hot buttons? What makes you run for the exits versus napping through the local happenings?

People prefer neighborhoods away from gunfire, and murder, rape and larceny. This is easier said than done as criminals have cars too. The best you can do is separate reality from perception and do the research. Which neighborhoods have less crime versus more? Those with more should move lower on your list of potential places to call home - no matter the qualitative side saying it's fine. It's not fine. Reduce your family's exposure to major crime areas as much as possible.

Domestic Mobility

Everyone is from somewhere- no exceptions. Being from a place doesn't mean, automatically, that you wish to remain from that place. Millions of people will live and die within twenty miles of their birthplace (almost 60%). Then there is everyone else: those adventurous souls willing to move to the next county (county, not country)! Some are willing to move even further from their place of birth: to another state. Fewer still are willing to consider relocation to a different part of the country, to places where the local customs are foreign (Ohio where chili includes spaghetti or a southern state where tea is sweet or un-sweet).

Moving, or relocating, has significant ramifications for families as people realize the further they move from "home" (the place of their birth) the fewer family members there are close by. Making new friends is never easy and finding new service providers is a requirement of modern living (doctors, dentist, and places of worship). Most people reading this book can slide right past these initial challenges because of remaining close to their original geographic roots. How many people have you met that grew up in western Massachusetts and now live in Colorado? Probably not many and that's just the way it is. Now for the hard part.

The Places in Your Life

Do you have children? You probably have strong opinions about where they should attend school. If this is a focal-point, then the geography is already narrowed for you based on school districts and maybe even publically available test scores produced by a school district. Some parents are hell-bent on selecting a school with a reputation for high graduation rates AND high college entrance exam scores.

Think about the places in your life; places of worship, favorite parks, where friends congregate and where your comfort level is at its peak. Does this guide you towards a certain part of the city? Are there multiple neighborhoods to consider? Are you excited about the possibilities?

Neighborhood Boundaries & Submarkets

Begin to narrow your search by reviewing submarkets. Submarkets are boundaries that define property with similar attributes. These same attributes can be useful to distinguish one area from another for a residential purchase. The term submarkets are applied most often to commercial property where the term neighborhood relates to residential property. Both terms are used to define an area by property use (zoning) and boundaries (streets and natural barriers).

For example, Dallas, TX has 38 submarkets; areas that are distinguished by certain distinct characteristics that make each place unique in the world. The City of Los Angeles has over one hundred distinct neighborhoods. A sub-market is:

- An area with similar properties in terms of physical housing stock and rents
- An area that reflects patterns of locational preference
- An area with defined transportation patterns, natural barriers
- Represents a profile of residents and workforce

This information continues to bring a rich layer of distinct information to a neighborhood that makes it unique as compared to other neighborhoods. This can include physical and demographic characteristics such as; architecture, street widths, foliage, ethnicity, household income and access to public transportation.

Decisions that Bubble

Think about and develop your viewpoint about place using the location-specific prompts outlined within this book and certain places will miraculously bubble up from the myriad of choices.

You know you are on the right track when ten or twenty potential neighborhoods narrows to three or five. As these neighborhoods begin to "bubble up" your affinity for one or two will increase even more as the search begins to narrow.

Decide on the exact neighborhoods that are acceptable places to purchase your home. You and no one else must predetermine this. These neighborhoods must meet your criteria. Granted, the number of neighborhoods can expand or contract based on new findings, however, the initial list must be of your design.

Yes, market forces (availability of housing stock, mortgage pricing) and price have a role in the never-ending argument in debate about where you want to live versus where you can afford to live. These arguments (in your mind) must finally come to an end here with a choice of neighborhoods that are acceptable, from a lifestyle perspective, and affordability.

Well, what if I am new to an area and have no clue? This is even more reason to explore and reach conclusions on your own with the input of your new local friends, co-workers and church members. Talk to strangers in coffee shops, dry cleaners or grocery stores. Ask the Produce manager about good neighborhoods.

Stop in fire stations, diners and locally owned businesses- they've been there for years. Tell people you are new to the area and are looking for a little guidance from people that know the place better than you do. You will be surprised at the engagement and willingness to help. Make an appointment with local police and Sheriff offices and have a short list of pertinent questions.

Many people believe they know exactly where they want to live. Just like love, you may think there is only a single soul in the entire universe right for you. Yet, there are probably a few additional choices to consider given a little more time to consider your options.

I am asking you to expand your thinking in terms of multiple neighborhoods that represent areas offering all the amenities and personal factors you have considered such as drive times, child services and community engagement. Allow yourself to discover new places and be surprised.

Having one neighborhood and only one will require much patience on your part; waiting for a home to come up for sale, hoping it is the "right" home and affordable. Having several potential neighborhoods provides broad choice, selection and comparison opportunities.

Action Steps

- Look at geography from street level- every house is on a street, in a neighborhood, in a city, in a county, in a state, in a country.

- Are you mobile? Can you, will you, move away from family to a "foreign place". For some people "far away" means the other side of town. What does mobility mean to you and what is your distance parameter?

- Know peak and off peak drive times to the places you visit most often- before you buy.

Website References:

- ESRI.com - Mapping for Everyone

- Bureau of Labor Statistics- Maps

- Homefair.com - City Profile Reports

Chapter 6: Step 6
Living the Life: Finding that Perfect Place

This book is intended to reduce some of the drama in the decision-making process. So many times "drama" is caused by procrastination. There is a systematic method for going through the paces in narrowing your choice of place. You must come to a decision, a quality decision. In part, that means avoiding an impulse purchase.

This is unlike when the salesman says to the happy couple "how would you like to pay for your purchase" and the couple give each other "that look" – the look that says, "wait, we are buying this thing?" As if they were just informed of the decision. You can't let a home sneak up on you. Certainly, it can happen. Try and narrow those occurrences to happy events rather than home-buyer's remorse.

Decision Points

Like many big decisions, buying a home is comprised of many small decisions rolled up into one big decision. Many of these aspects are discussed in prior chapters. In this chapter, we discuss the decision-points that encompass the place you will call home.

Decide on home size. How much home do you need and why? If you could have any size home, what would it be? When we get to cost, you can become practical, but for now think about your space needs only.

Some people will choose a closet-sized home in their absolute favorite neighborhood over a fabulous over-sized home somewhere else. These zealots are the happiest with their purchase decision. They are committed and bull-headed about their place of choice.

Is there room for compromise? Do you need or want to compromise? How far apart is perfect and near perfect? In home buying and life perfect seldom occurs. There should be "some" elasticity in your wish list to be real and allow for a pleasant surprise. You may discover that a picture-perfect deck or balcony with a beautiful view steals your heart and softens the fact that the kitchen is smaller than most. There will always be trade-offs to consider.

Is price the sole determinant? For many people the answer is no. In establishing price, there are probably numerous neighborhoods that will fit your pocketbook. Yet the question about where remains unanswered. Of course, you can purchase a home close to your favorite coffee shop but the other pieces of life revolve around a broader spectrum of activities than morning coffee.

Pick Three

To add some glue to the process, select three things that are must haves and three things that are an absolute no. This is always an evolving list- until it's not. It may take five or ten home tours in the process to make a solid list. And, the list may only have two items or expand to five. The longer the list the harder to find that perfect place meeting your criteria. The list is a guide to make "top of mind" those things that address your personal hot buttons. The list is there to reference when you "fall in love" with a place only to find out it doesn't meet any of your Pick Three requirements.

Here is an example of three must have positives:

1. Sunlight- big windows letting in light.

2. Attached garage parking- just easier to bring things in and out of the house.

3. Low traffic street. I want to be "off the beaten path" (in the cut) just a little.

And three absolute negatives:

1. Nowhere near a freeway. Just no. Prefer not to hear the constant hum of traffic.

2. A neighborhood with lots of boats, RV's and trailers parked in front yards. They become fixtures and part of the daily view.

3. Congested street parking. So many cars that even visitors will have a hard time coming to visit our house.

Do some brainstorming here and list those things that are important to you. For some there is nothing better than peaceable enjoyment- just quietness. Another family wants easy access to the airport. Another a place for the old family heirlooms to display. While everyone is a little different your choices for positives and negatives need to be in writing for reference. It is ok if they change over time, but there needs to be a starting point to guide the search process.

That Perfect Place

Where did you grow up? Urban or rural there is a place (or places) that bring memories of home. What are they and what do they represent? Collectively, they are more than just a single address. There is home and places close to home that represent home; the corner store, your favorite burger joint, the place to buy socks; your church and school. Maybe it's a park or favorite walking trail. These places (near home) represent a sense of place.

Yet people change. There are many city-dwellers that have moved to the burbs' or farther out and like it just fine. And just as likely there are country-raised people living in glass hi-rises in the city.

Try and think through making the perfect place a reality that fits your current and future lifestyle. Try not to settle.

About one in ten family's own a second home. So, that means most of us only get one therefore it's very important to review more than just the home itself and include neighborhood, commute times and access to places visited regularly. City-Data.com is a great website that drills down several layers into neighborhoods. It's easy to get lost and roam around this website. Remember to stay focused on the neighborhoods under consideration for your home.

It's perfectly fine to purchase a new(er) tract home that has limited to no personality but plenty of uniformity. It's what we do. But many people want a home that has some age, character and uniqueness. On that note, consider the following a window into just how much character you want to buy into and just how much uniqueness.

History and Reputation

Study the history of the place. The place where Al Capone died continues to exist with that incident as part of its history. Does that historic fact influence home value? Do homes close to Gettysburg or Kennesaw suffer the weight of historic events? The United States has a very short history. There are places in England where the "new bridge" is a mere one hundred years old. Gentrification in the United States often refers to "mid-century" homes... homes built in the 1950's. I'm just suggesting digging a little deeper than learning when the new big-box stores came into the neighborhood. There is always a history.

Gain an understanding about the reputation of a place. Every place has a reputation. Even if the reputation is that "nothing happens here" inquire further to determine the meaning of "nothing". If there are empty fields next to the subdivision growing onions and garlic nothing happens there excepting a real strong odor for several months a year.

Are You OK with That?

What are the things you want close to your home that make a difference to daily life? Are running or cycling paths a feature for the family? Some people love to ride their bicycles while others prefer an environment where there are always people coming and going- strollers and dogs everywhere.

Schools are important. A quality school system has a positive effect on property values. In fact, the reputation of a school district can have a dramatic impact on home valuations. While this is simple to say, it is difficult to validate and quantify; but make no mistake-- it is real. The best way to validate this is by checking graduation rates, college entrance exam test scores and talk to people that have a history with the schools such as retired teachers. They will tell you the real deal.

Traffic and School Traffic. Traffic is everywhere in an urban environment. School traffic is everywhere there is a school- and there are a lot of schools. It's one thing to have to slow or maneuver around the low speeds or backed up minivans. We all do this as part of being responsible adults, it's quite another thing to make school traffic part of your daily living experience because of proximity to school grounds. There are varying degrees of school traffic depending on the use. Grades K through 12 are daylight hours. Technical schools and Junior Colleges can have

58

activity from morning until late night with Learning Centers (or job centers) the same. Be aware of their proximity to your new home and consider the traffic patterns they create and when.

Pet Friendly. What exactly does "pet friendly" mean? Some neighborhoods are just chockfull of dogs; dogs and more dogs. If you are a dog lover, this may be fine with you. If you are not a dog lover this could be a problem. Like the neighbor that has fourteen go-carts in their front yard all the time, make inquiries about the local pet population. This same person may have fourteen dogs-one for each go-cart.

Pet friendly cuts both ways. There are pet lovers and pet haters. The two seldom cohabitate so why make it an issue with home buying? There are neighborhoods all over the country where people have pets that only live outside and others where Little Bullet-head sleeps on the pillow next to the homeowner. You pick- just get in there and know what you are buying into.

Sometimes your nose and ears will provide direct insight to the volume of pets. This is one of those qualitative areas as you can't get a count per se, but you can try and get a feel for the place. Get out of your car and walk around. An over-supply of pets can affect your living space and comfort level within the neighborhood.

Drive around the neighborhood after work and on weekends. It is good to know if your soon-to-be neighbors care about leash laws and picking up after their wayward animals or if they roam unleashed all the time. I am being not anti-dog. I am anti-unsupervised dog. While I want to know stray from domesticated I've never met a dog that could tell me about its vaccinations.

Crime statistics. Always review crime statistics. Crime is bad we all agree yet some crime is far worse than others. Crime against people is worse than crime against property. Some crimes fall into both categories- like home invasion.

Review crime statistics to gain as much information as possible about crime at and around the address of your potential purchase. Add to this the incidence of crime within proximity to the address. Then segregate the type of crime beginning with the most offensive; murder, forcible rape, attempted murder, muggings. This is uncomfortable but there is no one else to hand this task. Go to the local police station, Sheriff's office, State Troopers. If you walk in, go during non-peak times and tell them why you are there; I am looking to purchase my first home and I want to live in a safe and decent neighborhood. Be respectful of their time. It is amazing what you will find out and how open and honest the response.

Sex offenders are people too and they must live somewhere. We don't colonize people for criminal acts. That doesn't solve the problem. A multitude of government sponsored websites offer society a place to view where sex offenders reside. Don't let this freak you out when searching for a home. Look at the wide-view map. It's a lifetime felony. Consider that many offenders committed their offence years ago and never since. I am not excusing the behavior, just pointing out that for those non-repeat offenders they retain the labeling long after probationary periods have ended.

Saturday Night! Sunday Evening. Always drive by the property you intend to purchase on a Saturday night and a Sunday night. Here is why: Is the street party central or quiet as a mouse? It's a free country, anyone can throw a party at their home. Before you purchase a home, you just want to know if this is a nightly or weekly event, right?

Street Parking. There is not a lot you can do about street parking except make sure to know the ground and understand the "real deal". Is street parking allowed in front of your newly purchased home? What are the restrictions? Is street parking easily available or non-existent? Is there a time limit for parking? What happens to abandoned vehicles; are they addressed by the city or does it take a petition to get action? Do people care?

A street I travel on often has a 1960's Volkswagen parked on the street under a car cover. I would testify in court that this vehicle is a fixture having not moved in more than ten years.

I can recall having neighbors that while having available parking in front of their home parked in front of mine- blocking the mail box. A conversation solved the issue but it isn't always that easy. The point being check how things work on that street in real-life, day-to-day with respect to street parking.

Cultural centers and tourist. Many places across the country attract people to enjoy and engage a certain cultural or historical events. They are part of our heritage and identity. We cherish many of these sites and support them with our tax dollars. That does not necessarily mean you want to move in next to one. How close it too close? Each has a sphere of influence that affects its surrounding neighborhood. In some instances, this can be a few short blocks and in other instances several miles. When considering a home close to a cultural or tourist center determine its sphere of influence and the impact of visitors on your daily living experience.

Sports and concert venues. Are these close by and will they affect your "quiet enjoyment"? Because you like flowers is no reason to own a flower shop and having an affinity for the local sports team doesn't translate into wanting them and their fanatical fan's in your ear or trying to park on your front lawn. Where are these venues in proximity to your home and will the events held at the stadiums, theaters and ball parks impact your choice of place?

Weather and Weather Events. A community brochure can read "the average temperature is seventy-two degrees' year around. The brochure fails to mention that winter averages fifty degrees and the summer average is one hundred degrees. With a review of weather forget about averages by year and review averages by season. What is the average high and low temperature in spring, summer, winter and fall? If you are a local born and bred in a place, then you already know. For a home one-hundred miles away from a place you know, consider a weather review to compare. In California, for example, the changes in temperatures from the low desert to the high desert are dramatic.

Action Steps

- Pick Three must have's – really really really want these things in my new home.
- Pick three no go's – wouldn't buy it for a dollar.
- What attributes will a neighborhood have that makes it your perfect place?

Website References:

- City-data.com
- Family Watchdog.us
- Neighborhood Scout.com

Chapter 7: Step 7
Choosing your Home Buying Team

The primary members of your home-buying team include your real estate representative, legal counsel and lender. Your home-buying team are those people necessary to engage for purposes of purchasing a home.

Ominously excluded from your team in this chapter are the people engaged to assist in guiding your over-all financial planning. The home buying process should occur only after consultation with your financial planner and accountant "before" engaging the home-buying team.

No man, woman or potential homeowner is an island; you can't buy a home by edict or by command or wishful thinking. It takes a team of people, preferably people selected to assist you through the process and that have your best interest at heart. Team members, those selected for your home-buying team, should be people of character, whose opinions you trust and that have real world skills.

Why is the chapter on team so near to the back of the book? Shouldn't these people be with me from day one and assist in the process all along the way? Other than your financial planner and/ or accountant the short answer is no. Reason why: because while the advice of team members is very important at the appropriate time, <u>at the end of the day they go home- to their home- not your home.</u>

You are not asking for their permission. You have a team to assist in getting you through the process with the highest level of expertise necessary to assure your objectives are met. The decisions you form about pursuing home ownership, where and with whom is your decision. Having made the decision to proceed with homeownership your selected team members can assist you in getting there. That is their role.

Think about your last big purchase; a car, flat-screen television or vacation. How many resources did you use? Internet, friends, family, reviews- all good. How many people did you talk to before making the buying decision on that "big" purchase? Well, buying a home is a much bigger decision and will require other people to assist you through the process. The difference is that this decision is a very personal one.

So, while other people may have an opinion, at the end of the day, they go home (repeat intended). And most of them do not go home with you. The people that should have the most influence in this decision- the home buying decision- should be the adults living at the physical new address that occurs upon the end-result of this decision.

The following people, chosen by you, can make the process much easier than ever attempting to go it alone in the home buying process; representation, legal counsel and lender.

Representation

I am not a Realtor; however, I do recommend using a licensed real estate broker or agent. It's just easier for you. There are a million of them coast-to-coast, literally, one million to choose from. The good news here is that in your metro area you can interview Realtors until you find the right one. Some specialize in a certain property type, some by geography. Realtors represent the spectrum of humanity so look for one that compliments your perspective. Finding an agent that agrees with you all the time or is in constant pressure mode isn't focused on the prize.

Look for representation with compatible skills, someone who gets you, a representative willing to work with you for the long hall.

Ask your representative to provide standardized contracts and offer documents so you may familiarize yourself with them prior to having them placed in front of you for signature. Reading a Contract to Purchase Real Estate is a little easier when not actually purchasing real estate that very day.

Pay close attention to the binding nature of the contract and the disposition of earnest money at stake. If there are parts of the agreement you do not understand or where further clarity is required now is the time to ask those questions of your representative and attorney.

As an alternative, if your purchase is an off-market property, then please, without hesitation, engage a real estate attorney to assist with the purchase. There is too much money at stake (your money) to have an off-handed or laissez-faire (definition: letting things take their own course) approach to the contractual nature of a real estate purchase.

A word about Home Inspection Services. Best to seek a referral from your representative. Hiring a home inspector is placed under representation because this person on your team should have significant first-hand knowledge about the best people to hire for the type of property under consideration. They know who is good, honest and timely.

Legal Counsel

Everyone that is a party to the home sale and purchase will have legal counsel and you should also. Work of a multitude of attorney's is solidly at the table within the documents presented. Your representative has legal counsel, your lender has legal counsel, we can presume the seller does. And no one mentioned has cause to assure that YOU have representation.

Pre-closing (days before closing, not hours before) have your attorney review closing documents. Many people will tell you that all the paperwork is standard or normal, yet there is always an exception, a change. Here is an example.

Many properties have utility easements that "run with the land". They allow the electrical company or municipality to carry out their business without interruption of individual property owners for normal operations and maintenance, on power lines, for example. Most of these easements have a length and width described in the legal description of the property. What if the utility easement is 100 feet in width and runs from the back of the lot all the way to your back door? Wouldn't you want to know this?

While easements are common, those that are out-sized for any reason should be known to you pre-purchase. Flood plain maps, blemishes on title that are material, are best explained to you by your attorney. Only your attorney is compelled to share this information at the level of detail necessary to know if the issue impacts current and future value. Having your own legal counsel, a legal perspective set of eyes and ears, is integral to your success.

Lenders

Most mortgage lenders sell the debt (the mortgage) once the loan closes. They sell the loan immediately. Some local lenders retain servicing agreements that allow you to make your payment at a local branch. A local lender may keep the servicing (processing of payments) and a record of payments (a payment record or amortization schedule) sending your payments on to the actual owner of the mortgage.

There are a multitude of lenders in the mortgage market. And like with auto insurance many are exclusively online with promises of saving time and fees. In my experience, there is zero savings in time and limited (if any) savings in money by engaging an internet-only lender. As this is your first real estate purchase it's important to obtain as much hand-holding as possible so find a knowledgeable person to do business with in your local market. Many national lenders have local offices across the country so you don't have to sacrifice service.

There are several other service providers in addition to representation, legal and lender. We have already mentioned your accountant or financial planner. They are with you long before and long after this single transaction. Their input is your cornerstone for making the home buying decision. There is also the title company, home inspector, pest company, foundation review.

Title companies insure good transferable title. Title companies are like the American auto industry; you have a few good choices, but just a few. Most lenders have preferred title companies as do real estate representatives. If you have any concerns about the recommended title company, ask your real estate attorney for a thumb up or down as a double-check.

The home inspection company is a necessary component to learning as much as possible about the property and the remaining life of major systems including roofing, electrical, plumbing and heating. Ask if the home inspector is certified to review foundations. The pest inspection company is looking for any adverse conditions from current or former termites.

Action Steps:

- Ask your accountant and financial planner for referrals for your home buying team.

- Choose a real estate representative that understands your objectives and timeline.

- Establish a relationship with a real estate attorney to be on your team. Must be a real estate attorney- not an attorney that can spell real estate but without practical experience in the field.

Website References:

- Bankrate.com - 7 Tips For Picking A Real Estate Agent

- U.S. News.com Red Flags to Watch for When Picking a Real Estate Agent

- Zillow.com - Agent Finder

Chapter 8: Step 8
Home Loan Financing

This chapter is about home mortgage financing. At this stage, you have decided on certain neighborhoods and selected your team. Now it's time to look at available home financing options. As a potential homeowner, it is imperative that the person buying the home has the most say about the outcome. This includes being squarely in charge of selecting the best financing option.

In the United States, we are accustomed to the 30-year mortgage. It's a been around for generations now. In Japan, a popular loan is the "Flat" 35 with equal payments over thirty-five years. In Sweden, recently, the maximum mortgage term was cut from 140 years to 105 years. While that may seem unorthodox the reasoning is based on limited home affordability; home affordability was so low that the government changed lending rules to accommodate.

Credit markets are elastic and built on the interaction between GSE's (Government Sponsored Entities), lending institutions and consumers sentiment. Home pricing is elastic and has much to do with consumer sentiment and the availability of mortgage financing. In times of economic stress (regionally, nationally, internationally) people pull back from making big investments such as homeownership. The price of a home is indelibly tied to how they feel about the future, affordability and the availability of mortgage financing.

A young couple has decided to make the leap and search for a home. They are both recently out of college and have their heart set on a certain type of house close to a park. The savings they have are in good shape and Mom & Dad will add a little extra to the down payment if necessary. They make an appointment with a local lender who tells them that their dream home is out of reach and they should consider renting for another five years.

Devastated, they give up on homeownership based on the opinion of a single lender.

What's wrong with this picture? Meeting with a single lender that renders an off-handed opinion about what they can or cannot afford is folly and not fact. Yes, mortgage financing is important. What is more important is following all the steps leading up to deciding on whether to pursue home-ownership. Gaining quality advice from multiple sources is very important.

Too many people allow the loan process to drive their decision-making about homeownership. This young couple skipped a few steps along the way. First and foremost, they should have talked with their financial advisors to obtain a clear picture about their financial condition. A loan officer is not a financial advisor- they work for the lender- not you. This young couple made a life decision based on incomplete information provided by a single potential service provider (lender). This occurs all the time. They skipped important steps leading up to talking with a lender.

Skipping team guidance has resulted in too many people relying on hearsay without the guidance of people that understand their current objectives and long-term financial goals. Always true: other people will gladly have an opinion about where you should live and how much you can spend on a home.

Seeing Clearly

Obtaining a mortgage is very paper intensive. The lender will require a small boat-load of paperwork from you. The best way to understand what the lender requires is to ask; ask for their borrower checklist of required documents. Review the checklist with the lender to gain clarity about what they need and when they need it.

Preparation eliminates panic. Don't panic. Don't procrastinate. Be ahead of the curve in your preparation and documentation for the lender. Mortgage financing is not a game of hide-and-seek. If you are a qualified borrower the lender wants to assist in any way they can while assuring you and the property meets or exceeds lender underwriting standards.

The good news is that preparation can eliminate panic in the mortgage approval process. For your own sanity, and to remove the mystery from home loan financing, you will be devoting time to meetings with your accountant and financial advisor. Notice I did not say banker or mortgage broker. Yes, at this point they need to be on your radar screen, but communication for purposes of securing a home loan comes "after" you have a clear understanding of your financial situation from the financial advisors engaged to assist with your overall financial situation (your accountant and financial planner). Let me explain.

If you have $25,000 a prudent financial advisor will tell you that placing $24,000 towards the down payment of a house increases your financial risk. Every financial advisor I have ever listened to suggest having three to six months living expenses in cash on-hand for life's emergencies. Cash towards a down payment should be accumulated on top of this reserve. And there is the big Y in the road.

A banker or real estate sales advisor, seeing you have $25,000 cash towards the purchase of a home would not hesitate to have you commit this entire amount towards the purchase of a home. The banker and real estate advisor are both service providers being paid for services rendered. They only get paid if there is a transaction- so the more transactions they participate in the better.

Your financial advisor is hoping for a relationship with you for life, well beyond any single transaction. A good financial advisor will have your long-term interest at heart. Many service providers are gone forever the day after closing. Some have a longer-term perspective, of course. The smart ones know you will be looking for a newer or bigger home in a few years.

Listen and collaborate with your financial advisors. Fold in service providers on an as-needed basis after there is a plan of action in place that takes your long-term financial goals into consideration.

As a homeowner staying in one place for many years presents the opportunity to own a home debt free. Having a home free and clear of debt means having purchased a home with a mortgage and paying it down to zero. For many, the objective is to pay off their home on or before retirement knowing that household income will likely be less in retirement. Thus, long-term planning allows some homeowners to enter the retirement years without a mortgage payment.

Preapproved vs Pre-qualified

A banker or mortgage banker is in the business of making loans. The role of the banker is to produce business (home loans) for their respective employer of which you are a potential customer. If you qualify for a loan, of course, they are ready and willing to proceed. And as much as they are aware of your overall financial condition based on the loan application, they are unaware, and uncaring about your lifetime financial plan.

Your personal financial and investment advisors are your 'secret weapon" against the outside world. This is just as true when it comes to home buying and the mortgage lending process. With your collaboration, your advisors understand your overall financial goals, plans and what it takes to get there. Your financial advisors; spouse, accountant, financial planner or portfolio manager are keenly aware of your financial condition and should absolutely have a hand in guiding the financial decision-making process towards sound financial decisions including the impact of purchasing a home and obtaining a mortgage loan. This is true at any level and keenly important when looking to become a first-time homeowner.

Within this book steps on the path to purchasing a home are ordered; there is no reason to contact a lender prior to finishing the steps above this chapter. This includes making the decision to buy, deciding on property type, reviewing neighborhoods; do all these things prior to contemplating financing or focusing on mortgage financing.

Having a "pre-approved" or "pre-qualified" lender letter in hand too soon throws off the entire process. It will practically demand you go straight from the lenders office to looking at homes for sale. After all, there is an "expiration date" on the letter. Well big whoop. Who wants to get married after just two dates one of which was in a movie theater? Please do not let a lender letter derail the home buying process. Follow the steps within these pages- in order.

Obtain mortgage loan approval only when you are prepared to make written offers on homes

If the lender letter is for an amount less than the requested loan necessary to make the purchase the lender is basically telling you that their underwriting will allow you to borrow no more than the stated amount- from them. If there is a gap between the amount requested and the loan amount needed to close the sale, you will need to increase your down payment for the lender to make the loan or consider homes at lower price points (or consider using a different lender). This is an over-simplification as every lender is different, however, the lender should be able to express the reasoning behind their maximum loan amount if it is less than the amount requested.

For many people the clock starts ticking on a home purchase once they contact a lender. Loan approval has its place in the home buying process; after completing your neighborhood assessment. Obtaining loan approval prior to taking the time to think through and investigate neighborhoods right for you will create undue pressure to eliminate the neighborhood assessment altogether and just start looking at homes. What's wrong with that? Everything. Everyone wants to rev up the hunt at this point. Hold up. Slow down. Wait. Follow the steps. Do your assessments, drive the neighborhoods, get statistics, walk the sidewalks.

There are two very different primary forms of lender letters; one is a mortgage loan pre-approval letter, the other is a pre-qualification letter from the lender. In many circles these are the same thing. The distinction between them is subtle yet real. Let's look at both.

Pre-Approval

Every lender you meet will share that the best way to purchase a home is to obtain pre-approval for a home loan before looking for a home to purchase. These are the rules. This is tradition. This is wrong. This is wrong because obtaining that pre-approved loan starts the clock ticking. Every pre-approval states clearly that this pre-approval has an expiration date.

Following is a single paragraph within the atypical preapproval letter:

> *This preapproval is not a commitment to lend. You will need to finalize your mortgage application, and we will need to verify your information and review your financial documentation before we can decide on your application. A loan commitment also depends on property acceptability and eligibility, including the appraisal and title report. Preapprovals are subject to change or cancellation if your requested loan no longer meets applicable regulatory requirements.*

This paragraph is buried in the letter after the header that reads CONGRATUALATIONS – YOU ARE PRE-APPROVED! So even though this paragraph outlines multiple necessary actions before an actual approval people take this to mean their loan is approved. Wrong. At best, it is a conditional approval which is nothing more than the lender representing that you have passed the sniff test and they are willing listen and learn and let you tell them more.

Yet, to the world at large having a mortgage pre-approval letter in hand means you are ready to pull the trigger NOW. Once the mortgage pre-approval letter is in hand EVERYONE presumes an offer on a home is forthcoming. Yet, the language clearly states that additional information will be required including verification of financial documentation. A pre-approval letter states that you have passed the first bar of many bars in the loan processing.

Pre-Qualification

Gaining information on what lenders may lend based on an overview of your financial condition is accomplished with pre-qualification. Lenders require a completed and signed loan application for pre-qualification. Having a mortgage loan pre-qualified means an applicant has submitted all documents required for the lender to make an initial credit decision. The lender has invested the time necessary to assure the information is true and correct (validated) and issues a letter to the borrower that they are "pre-qualified" for the loan amount stated on the lenders letterhead. The lender has reviewed (and validated) the financial information presented in making this decision.

With a mortgage pre-approval letter your mortgage application requires completion. With a pre-qualification letter your mortgage application is complete and the financial information therein validated. You are closer to becoming a home-owner with a pre-qualification letter in hand.

Fixed versus Variable Rate Mortgages

Nothing makes us more uncomfortable than HUGE swings in interest rates. We humans are creatures of habit and we prefer stability; we want to know that the price of something yesterday will remain the same tomorrow. Upset our apple cart on this and we get uneasy. The higher the price spike in a product the more uneasy we get.

I would like to say that a fixed rate mortgage is always better than a variable rate mortgage but that would be an untrue statement. In times when fixed rate mortgages are at eighteen percent a variable rate mortgage has its place and can be a great value. In a low rate environment obtain a fixed rate mortgage and please remember; home equity is not a cash machine to draw on at will.

Variable rate financing has its place in the home-buying marketplace. Often it will allow first-time homeowners to gain access to debt financing at levels they can't reach with a fixed rate mortgage. Bottom line: use a variable rate mortgage as necessary to buy your first home, but migrate to a fixed-rate mortgage as soon as possible. Note that some mortgages have lock-out periods (a period when the loan cannot be pre-paid). This is more common with variable rate mortgages so you may have to keep the loan for several years before being able to refinance with a fixed-rate mortgage.

Part of the process of obtaining a mortgage loan is the lender's analysis of your financial condition including income, credit quality and down payment capacity. The more cash you have in the deal, miraculously, the better qualified an applicant becomes. While the length of the loan may remain the same the interest rate and fee structure will vary significantly; the higher the down payment, the better the loan terms with respect to interest rate. The ability of a new homeowner to gain the best pricing on the loan (the best interest rate) begins with a twenty-percent cash down payment. Anything less and the lender will require additional fees and insurances to make the loan.

A word about impound accounts: many lenders require an impound account to collect money with your mortgage payment towards the annual expense of taxes and insurance. While this is often standard operating procedure there are always exceptions so please avoid assumption, and make sure to know if impounds for taxes and insurance are collected with the loan payment. Make a note to know who (which institution) is responsible for making these payments in a timely manner.

Will your loan require mortgage insurance? This is a big deal and the rules change often. The bottom line is if the cash down payment is less than twenty percent of the purchase price then your lender may require (meaning it's not even remotely optional) mortgage insurance. This is referred to as PMI insurance, or Principal Mortgage Insurance. This insurance protects the lender in case of default. It is very expensive and only protects the lender (not you). Lenders are required to drop the PMI insurance once the equity in the home is more than twenty-two percent (22%).

A Note About Home Equity

Lenders will be lenders. Lenders have a continuous stream of advertising targeted to homeowners that convey that your home equity is available for any purpose. The advertising suggests that home equity loans are there for the taking and you too should enjoy the fruits of your labor with immediate gratification with a new thirty-year mortgage attached.

Here is the real deal; equity is a gift and not a right. Home equity that you have earned over the course of time is no fickle thing to throw at a vacation or new car purchase. Becoming a homeowner brings a certain level of satisfaction and security, yes? So, this very same place is not to be utilized like an automated teller machine for whimsical purchases.

In the chapter entitled "Know Your Exit Strategy Before Buying" I stated that your home is not real estate. This was to get you into the frame of thinking about your home as something other than a financial endeavor for gain. Recognize, please, that your home is also not a credit card with a roof. While home equity loans have their place, frivolous spending for short-term pleasures negates all you have worked for with respect to homeownership.

Action Steps:

- Allow your financial advisors (your accountant and financial planner) to drive the process and work with you to determine a reasonable level of mortgage financing that "fits" with your overall financial plan.

- Preparation eliminates panic. Don't panic. Don't procrastinate. Be prepared and ahead of the curve in your preparation and documentation for the lender. Ask questions.

- Understand the difference between pre-approved and pre-qualified. Drive the process at a speed that works for you- do not let a lender hurry your home buying decision based on a date on a letter.

Website References:

- Freddie Mac.com - Step by Step Mortgage Guide for Single-family Homes

- Practical Money Skills.com - Life Events: Mortgage

- Investopedia.com - How to Select a Financial Advisor

- John Wilhoit.com – click on Home-Ownership for a free email course "10 Ways to Find Your Down Payment"

Chapter 9: Step 9

House Hunting - The Search Process

This chapter on house hunting is the longest chapter in the book. The goal of this chapter is to save you hundreds of hours and thousands of dollars in wasted time, energy and effort in pursuit of homes that are outside of your sweet spot, personally, financially or geographically.

Stay focused on what works for you. That means staying away from going to see homes that are "out of bounds" in any way. The term "looky lu" should never be applied to you- you do not have time to waste on such. Your goal is to find a home that fits the parameters set. Everything else is off the table.

For so many first-time home-buyers this is the hard part. How do I go about finding the house of my dreams? It is such a daunting task! The good news is that with this book you have already outlined all the phases to proceed. In the prior chapters, and by following the action steps, your home search is ready to begin. Think about it for a minute. While you were reading didn't you begin to think about buying or not buying, about exit strategy, property type, who will be on your team, the geography, demographics and finding that perfect place?

Sticking to Your Guns

Initially, the number of available homes will seem like an avalanche or a constant wave washing over you. There are just so many! However, as you apply the Twelve Steps to Homeownership the numbers will narrow immensely.

These are the steps you will have completed prior to house hunting:

- Making the decision to become a homeowner.
- Consider your exit strategy- before buying.

- Decide on a property type; single-family, townhome, condo or another type.

- A review of the demographics – an authentic look at the people selected as your future neighbors.

- A review of on-the-ground geography – selecting the where (see geo-funnel).

- Contemplation of lifestyle attributes – living life in a place selected by you.

- Choosing a team to accomplish the task of buying a home and discussions with your financial advisors.

- An initial discussion with a lender about home loan financing and becoming pre-approved or pre-qualified.

Having selected your geography, neighborhoods and housing type, be prepared to say no again and again. One of the pressures of home buying is that everyone is on a timeline. It's just the nature of the business. The sooner you buy something the sooner your service providers get paid. The sooner you buy the sooner they are released to service other clients having provided their services to you.

Think about placing an order at a fast food restaurant; the order taker could care less how long it takes a customer to place an order; they get paid the same no matter how long it takes. The store manager, however, standing behind the order taker is more than a little annoyed with slow ordering customers. The longer it takes a customer to order the longer the line gets as production slows and thin profit margins become even thinner.

There are many reasons to say no, one hundred times no. The primary reason will be when a property is presented to you that falls outside of your stated geography or property type. While it's nice to know about a condominium facing the golf course is available at a steal of a price, if your focus is on a suburban single-family home with a yard the condo is of no merit.

The nuances become difficult requiring you to stay true to your home buying premise. For example, when presented with a "cute as a button" two-bedroom having explicitly stated that three bedrooms are mandatory or stating your preference for an upper floor condo and the only one available is second floor. When the "picture perfect house" is brought to you a mere seventy-five thousand dollars over your stated budget. Surely the seller will come down some so let's go for it! Perhaps. Regardless, stay in your (financial) lane.

Flexibility Is Your Friend

Without changing a single word from the prior segment in this chapter, sometimes the most important factor you can bring to a transaction is time flexibility; the ability to close fast or extend the closing by weeks or even months. When a seller has two offers for the same dollar amount, the time factor can be the linchpin to gaining the property.

Is the seller in need of a quick close or wanting to stay in the house until the end of the school year? Can you accommodate? If the answer is yes, everything else being equal, then your offer goes to the head of the line. Some sellers, while wanting to sell, need to push the transaction into the next calendar year. If it is June, then that's a stretch for most people. If you can accommodate the seller, then again, your offer rises above all others.

Another form of flexibility comes in the form of <u>repairs</u> flexibility. If the home inspection identifies items that the seller should address, if your offer will accept the property with the noted flaws, then the home is closer to being yours. Suggesting acceptance if certain flawed items are found is far from rubber stamping an "as is" sale. I'm suggesting if the home has everything on your wish list, location, schools, commute time, architecture, and it just feels like "home" then it is up to you to make the deal work in your favor. This is just one small way to differentiate your offer from other potential buyers.

It could be simple things such as peeling paint, cracks in the driveway or missing doors, broken windows or a broken garage door. Far from saying these things are ok, I am suggesting that the dollar amount to remedy such is very small in comparison to gaining ownership of your dream home. Acceptance of such things also differentiates your offer from others that are requesting the property be delivered in picture perfect condition.

Find That House!

In the discussion about Team, having a real estate representative is suggested as they are the most plugged into the local market. Initially, you do have to select just one person. When selecting this person, you are choosing them AND the team they bring. In a perfect world, the selected person can provide the necessary services. However, just like any other service provider, you may have to fire one and hire another. This could range from recognizing they are not the right fit to having selected someone who is just too busy to provide the level of service you require.

The initial "cutline" on the table for areas to consider are the selected neighborhoods- those selected by you. This list will expand and contract some as the search narrows yet should always meet the criteria outlined, again- by you. Share this list with your real estate representative but do not make changes to it without cause. A knowledgeable real estate representative, once seeing your neighborhood list, will very likely recommend additional neighborhoods that seem to meet your described criteria. This is always a positive- to have an opportunity to explore places that you may have missed or never knew existed.

Neighborhoods versus Zip Codes

Neighborhoods take into consideration the methods outlined within these pages; lifestyle, demographics, crime statistics, etc. Zip codes have multiple business and route uses. A neighborhood may fit into a single zip code. More than anything, remember to stay in your lane; stay in the designated neighborhoods painstakingly selected. Change and refine search areas as new information becomes available. How often? As often as the new areas meet or exceed the outlined selection criteria.

Taking Notes

In a perfect world, the home search process begins in one month and ends in the next as that perfect place is found and bought. This is seldom the case as the process often requires kissing a lot of frogs before finding your prince or princess.

It is important to keep track of places visited. Create a file with the addresses visited and any unusual aspects about the place or its surroundings. This is important as people often circle back to a place a month or two later. Write down one or two big pro's and con's. It could be things about the house or the street. Here are some examples:

- 123 Main Street. Beautiful landscaping but expensive to maintain. Three car garage. Neighbor had five big dogs!
- 500 N. Maple. Very small kitchen but HUGE deck.
- 6 Pryor Court. I could hear the neighbors in the next condo talking in just a normal voice. Thin walls!

About FSBO'S, FIXER'S & REO'S

All such homes can potentially be on your list of potential homes to purchase. All require "extra" to get the deal done. They fall outside of the every-day buy-sell structure represented by having a broker, buyer and seller. In the case of For-Sale-By-Owner, there is often no broker involvement so the buyer and seller are left to figure it out for themselves (not you, of course, because you will have representation regardless). With Fixer's there is more work to do prior to move in and with Foreclosures and REO there are additional parties to the transaction that have a say in how the sale will proceed.

FSBO. For Sale by Owner (FSBO) homes are often independently advertised and not part of multiple list services. Agree to pay the fee to your representative if they bring you a FSBO. Yes, it increases your costs by a few percentage points. It also opens up the market just a little bit more. As we have discussed, homeownership is a lifetime and lifestyle decision. You will want to see all available inventory in your selected neighborhoods.

When hiring a real estate representative one form of employment is entitled "buyer's agent". This designation contractually outlines the representative is your exclusive agent for a set amount of time and that you have agreed to pay them a set fee (usually a percentage of purchase price) upon successful completion of the transaction. This form of contract is utilized by attorney's and real estate agents. My suggestion is to have the contract include payment of a fee for the purchase of a FSBO. If the agreed upon fee is three percent, for example, then you (the buyer) will pay this fee on top of the purchase price at closing.

FIXER'S. Fixer's or fixer-upper's are represented by homes available for sale where the cost of repairs represents some percentage of the sales price, usually ten percent or more. A bad example is a home that has a market value of $200,000 available for sale for $180,000 requiring $20,000 in repairs. In other words- it's no bargain. As a potential home-owner looking at this home you would bring your home inspector and a general contractor to assure you could accomplish the repairs for $20,000 or less. So why even consider such a home with all the extra work necessary to make it livable? There is only one reason…

If you were in the fixer-upper business there is zero profit potential in this home as represented. As a home-owner-to-be the only reason to consider this home is if it meets all your established purchase criteria; right size, amenities, location, schools, etc. The up-side is that the necessary repairs will allow for some customization along the way so you, the new home-owner, will have your imprint on the house from move in day! Paint, flooring, light fixtures- all selected by you.

The downside to buying a fixer is you will need to remain a renter concurrent with the work getting done and it will be necessary to find a lender willing to structure their mortgage as a purchase and construction loan. Moving into a fixer to then fix it is a scenario I wish on no one. Too much gets lost in translation; short cuts, short on dollars to finish the job right, rushing. Working around "everything".

A construction-purchase loan is not that difficult to secure if you meet the normal under-writing standards from a local lender. However, some may ask for a larger down-payment to offset the lenders construction risk. Those with the gold make the rules. That's just the way it is.

FORECLOSURES. Foreclosure and pre-foreclosure sales represented a pretty good percentage of homes last decade. With so many homes under water (meaning, having a mortgage balance higher that market value) there was an entirely new vocabulary established to deal with the volume of transactions. The operative word is "short sale".

A short sale requires the lender to agree to accept a payoff of the existing mortgage for an amount less that what is owed. The seller wants to sell and move, but owes more than the market value. If the bank agrees to take less that the amount owned the seller can sell and you can purchase the home. The benefit to the bank is that they recover X percent of their money without having to foreclose on the property only to end up with some similar amount from the sale months or years later.

A traditional foreclosure sale is often represented as an "as is" sale with the buyer taking on all risk of condition. The property many have been vacant for some time so it will require a meticulous inspection to assure all major systems are in good order.

REO. Real Estate Owned (REO) by a bank or other financial institution. These are homes owned by the bank and available for sale in as-is condition. As with fixers and foreclosures they are always sold in as-is condition so make sure to take the time for thorough inspections.

Passive Search

A passive search includes all activity leading up to stepping inside of a potential home for sale. While the sensory perception may seem limited, the work will ease the process immensely. Or said another way; surfing from the sofa. Great to do but by itself will never get the job done. I have personally made purchases above two million dollars from properties identified by a web search. Of course, this is just the first of many steps to making the purchase.

As of this writing the two websites for home searching online with the most listings are Zillow and Realtors.com. Also, check out Home Finder.com that list homes from newspapers around the country. Consider For Sale By Owner.com and Land and Farm. com. This is a starter list.

Active Search

Your active search is an extension of all the action steps completed prior including the passive search. Now it is time to step inside of your potential new home. It's time to physically go inside of homes available for sale. In the process of completing the Twelve Steps to Homeownership the funny thing is you will know when you've stepped inside your future home. There won't be any boxes to check or list to review; you've done all that. The search will have come to an abrupt halt.

Yes, there is still a checklist, an offer to make and get accepted by the seller, a loan to put in place- all the necessary busy work of scheduling inspections and coordinating the process. All part of the process to obtain that singular objective of buying your home, that place on the planet to call your own.

On your second read through this book focus on the action steps provided at the end of each chapter. The time to do this is at the front of the search process. Your second read through this book will serve to validate that you are on top of your game and tracking towards finding your home.

Action Steps:

- Check out neighboring homes and yard upkeep. Here is why: if your new neighbor has a bass boat and camper in their driveway under a blue tarp covered with pine needles chances are it will still be there five years from now.

- Use aerial maps as part of your property review before you buy. Here is why: aerial maps let you see things you simply cannot see from the ground. A web search will return various sources for local maps, however, the search and review only starts with the top three websites on the page. Local universities and governmental agencies will have maps allowing you to go deeper into the search results. Please do not discount these.

- Whereas it's nice to get the free stuff from the big search engines, local planning and zoning, county offices and the U.S. Geological Survey all have much to offer on a localized basis. Also, providing free mapping services to the public in some form: University Extension offices, USDA, Bureau of Land Management, NASA.

Website References:

- Zillow
- Realtors.com
- Home Finder.com

Chapter 10: Step 10
Making the Offer

Your game plan for making an offer is to deploy your team into position for writing a contract and presenting it to the seller for consideration. Making an offer on real estate is very paper intensive. Yes, e-signatures are in heavy use (at the time of this writing) yet at the end of the day someone (probably you) must sign an actual piece of paper with an actual ink pen. Welcome to 21st century progress!

As noted in the Chapter 7 - "Choosing Your Home Buying Team", prior to making an offer get copies of standard contracts and documentation from your real estate representative and review them at your leisure, long before making an actual offer; weeks or months before- so you can study the documents and get all your questions answered. Having done so the task of signing the contract once prepared for your signature will seem a little less overwhelming.

Reviewing the standard contract prior to use in real-life allows time to familiarize yourself with the documents, ask questions of your attorney and become aware of the fact that your earnest money is at risk from the date of signature on the contract until it is either released or applied to the purchase price of the home at closing.

Natural Next Step

Making an offer on a home is the natural next step to all the hard work performed to this point. Making the offer funnels all your efforts into the focal point of choosing a place. Like proposing marriage, making an offer presumes a wedding soon. The wedding "day" is closing day when you are officially a homeowner. Enjoy the moment.

Waiting on Perfection

Does the property meet your "Pick Three"? Go for it~! We can talk sports, cars, fashion or home buying, there is no such thing as perfection. Granted, while it is still a weighted decision, the Pick Three perfection can be negated by fifty-five negatives. But waiting on the "perfect" home, down to the infinitesimal floor finishes that glimmer in both sun and moonlight will only lead to frustration and shame. Yes, I said shame.

There will be ample people in your circle that deem you a failure in life if you seek and search for a home and come up empty (the shame!). Discretion is a necessary component of the home buying process and the offer stage is doubly so. Don't tell everyone your business.

I pray I have made it blatantly clear to not go it alone, but select good counsel near the beginning of the process and lean on these people to fulfill their respective roll as you delve deeper into the process and closer to making offers. If one or more people from your selected team are non-responsive or deliver poor recommendations- remove and replace with someone competent and willing to move forward.

I bring this up in the offer chapter because one thing is certain; if you make no offers you will buy no house. And the pressure can be amazingly high. It takes a lot of courage to wait on that one home that is a fit for you and your family. My point is to measure your emotions and try your best to stay sane. Making an offer is not for the weak of heart. Making an offer on the wrong house just to create the illusion of progress is wrong and places your earnest money at risk. You want to be happy in your new home and select the right one that is appropriately financed. Patience is a necessity.

Acceptance

Having an accepted offer is both exhilarating and terrifying; like being on a roller coaster without a seatbelt holding on tight seems the only way to survive. Yet the opposite is true. It's more like holding a golf club, gently yet firm. This is true because although you are in the eye of the storm there are certain protections in place, namely, the professionals including your lender and title insurance company. Neither firm will allow you to proceed unless their collateral is secure and title to the property is certain to transfer into your name.

Having an accepted offer sets into motion loan processing concurrent with the home inspection. Being pre-qualified for a home loan the lender is ahead of the curve since they have everything necessary to make a credit decision. The lender will order the appraisal and ask you for updates to some of the information previously provided.

The outcome of the appraisal will be delivered to the lender and you, the borrower. Assuming the numbers are in order, the lender will tell you the estimated date of closing. At this point, assuming the title work is without flaw, you are days away from being a homeowner.

Action Steps:

- Review standard contracts for making offers long before signing a "live" offer document. Ask legal counsel any questions you have and make sure you understand the documents signed for presenting an offer to buy real estate.

- Meet with your advisors and make sure everyone is aware a written offer in process - a live offer to purchase a home.

- Do not wait on perfection. Be nimble enough to adapt if the offer meets your "Pick Three" threshold.

Website References:

- U. S News.com - Rules to Live By When Making an Offer on a House

- Salary.com - First Time Home Buyer Tips: Making the Offer

- Realtor.com - The Basics of Making an Offer on a House

Chapter 11: Step 11

Home Inspection

Your home inspector will have a great brochure to convey what they do and how they do it and the outcome of their work. However, there are many things to review outside of the scope of the home inspection as a new homeowner.

Do not buy a home without hiring a professional home inspector. Here is why: A home inspection is highly recommended for the trouble they can save you. They provide a type of inexpensive insurance. The best way to gain the most from the inspection is to be familiar with the scope of work and terms used by the inspector. Knowing the vocabulary allows you to ask intelligent questions. The underlying reasoning is that this purchase will be your home purchased with your money.

The Home Inspectors List

The home inspector will review major systems including heat and air-conditioning, power and structural systems such as foundation and roofing. The detail is available for your review in sample reports prior to the inspection and in the subject property inspection report delivered post-inspection.

In selection of a home inspector consider their experience and licensing in related construction specialties such as engineering, mechanical systems, electrical or plumbing. You can also obtain referrals for your area from the American Society of Home Inspectors.

There is always a section entitled "findings" (or something similar). These are the items the inspector intends to bringing to your attention. They usually point out any significant deficiencies or items that require immediate corrective action. The items could be as small as peeling paint or as large as cracked rafters. Read the report in full, but pay special attention to "findings".

Your (Home Inspection) List

Many of the following items will be very important to you as the soon-to-be resident. Although they are often outside of the scope of the home inspection report they allow you to look, consider and review items that are important on move-in day. Here is a list of things you will want to know:

Year Built. Check this date in public records. Here is why: it is important to know the actual true age of original construction regardless of any structural updates. Original year of construction can be found in the appraisal. Properties that are twelve years and older could have experienced replacement of major systems- water heaters, roof, etc.

Quality of construction. This may seem subjective but a professional should be able to quantify the status in writing. This is where your home inspector earns their money as they measure the home "as built" and comment on any upgrades or improvements. Since this is somewhat subjective, cross reference the information from your home inspection with the information presented in the property appraisal.

Termite and Pest inspection. The termite and pest inspection is outside of the scope of most home inspectors. Your lender will require a termite inspection. However, if there is no loan required to purchase the home (an all cash transaction), please, still insist on a termite and pest inspection.

Cost of Utilities for this address. Always check the historic cost of utilities for the specific address you are buying. Obtain average utility usage for the last twelve months directly from the utility companies.

Utility and Internet service providers. Identify all available service providers, electric, water & sewer, natural gas, cable, internet, satellite. There is always a surprise about how many providers, or how few, there are for a specific address.

Paint Brands. Ask the seller about existing paint to find out the brand, age and composition; some are flat, some satin, etc. There are a thousand different "eggshell" colors depending on the manufacturer.

Cell Phone Signal Strength. Check cell phone signal strength inside and outside of the home. This is so easy to miss because we all take it for granted that our phones work everywhere.

Open every door and window to make sure they work. The home inspector may open and close many windows and doors, but not necessarily every window and door. The home inspector will look in the closets, but your things must fit in there so look inside.

Flooring and floor coverings. Most homes have multiple floor coverings from carpet to tile to vinyl products and wood. Consider what to keep and what to remove while the home is still empty of furniture.

Door widths. Standard door widths are 32 and 36 inches. Entry doors can be larger. Something to pay attention to with respect to accessibility.

Exterior lighting. Exterior lighting is an initial security measure with respect to safety and comfort in knowing that the property has proper lighting. Take note of what is in-place and areas that could benefit from additional lighting.

Landscaping. What is the monthly cost to maintain the existing yard? What low-cost improvements could be implemented right away? What can or should be removed from an esthetics perspective?

Decks and Steps. Considering the time of year do they require any immediate attention?

HVAC compressor platform. Although small it is important. It should be checked for stability, functionality and sturdiness.

Trees are important. Consider hiring a horticulturist to review the trees and plants on the property. Here is why: even on a small property there might be some valuable timber to cut and sell. After replanting consider using any remaining dollars to reduce your mortgage balance. Take note of trees that could cause damage to the home if they were to fall from wind or storms.

Action Steps:

- Obtain referrals for home inspection companies. Check their references and credentials.

- This entire chapter is an action step. The action step is completed once you have reviewed the completed home inspection report and addressed the findings with the seller and agreed on common ground remedy deficiencies.

- Use "Your (Home Inspection) Inspection" as a prompt to create a custom list appropriate for the property under consideration.

Website References:

- Total Home Inspection.com Total Home Inspection Checklist

- Gardening Solution - University of Florida - Landscaping for Specific Sites

- University of California - Integrated Pest Management Program - Pest Notes

Chapter 12: Step 12
Closing Day

It ain't over til it's over. Fat lady singing. Lights out. Whatever metaphor you want to use it's all true here. In my experience, most deals that "blow up" do so the week before closing. The seller changes their mind. There is a fire. The lender changes the terms. The happy couple buying the home file for divorce. You can't make this stuff up.

5! 4! 3! 2! 1!

Five business days until closing. What could go wrong? What is yet undone? What can you do to assure a low-key week leading up to closing versus hair-on-fire madness? It is important to remember several items can be accomplished days prior to assist in moving things along. For example, the final walk-through inspection can occur a day or three before closing.

Every deal is different. With the help of your team, complete a list of items to accomplish then prioritize them. Next, set them to a calendar: each-and-every item. Following are examples of items to accomplish in the days prior to closing day.

- 5 days from closing – Address those things hardest to correct or the most difficult to procure
- 4 days from closing – Confirm agreed upon repairs are done, review inspection reports
- 3 days from closing – Walk-through. Call locksmith and set appointment to change the locks and security codes.
- 2 days from closing – Prepare for moving day… collect tele numbers for utility companies, internet service, etc.
- 1 day from closing – A quiet day (hopefully).

Paperwork, paperwork

Everyone has paperwork for you; the real estate sales representative, lender, title company, home insurance provider and home inspector. While electronic copies are fine, at this stage there will be a requirement to sign certain documents by hand on paper. Be sure to retain a copy of any document you sign by hand. Every. Single. One. No exceptions. The paper trail has an end date, yes, but all along the trail there is the potential for revisions and changes to former originals.

Almost home!

At this point, your financing is in order (approved weeks prior) and inspections are in order. The lender may ask for updated bank statements. There is no need to panic although some serious anxiety is going on inside your head. You may flinch when the phone rings. Now breathe. Remember to breathe.

Have a closing day checklist of things to obtain from the seller. Very often your real estate representative will have collected the items a day or two before closing. You need keys, garage door openers, security codes, helpful phone numbers for trash pickup, lawn care, pool service and snow removal. Turn in a change of address from the Post Office. These make for a smooth transition into your new home.

Always double check closing statements. Here is why: Because people make mistakes. Seldom is the mistake intentional on a closing statement. Sometimes it's simple math or a transposed number providing a double credit to one side or the other.

Review mortgage loan documents. There is nothing fun about this part. The document is long, filled with legalese and all about what will happen if you default, pay late or otherwise lose your ability to make timely payments. Whereas the rights of the borrower are noted, the rights of the lender are spelled out and expressed in long-hand page after page.

Often, interest due on the very first mortgage payment is folded into the loan, therefore, the first mortgage payment to make is 31-59 days after closing. Read the closing documents closely to know when you must make your first mortgage payment.

Create a Closing File

Create a closing file because this house will sell again one day. When that occurs, your accountant will need to know the "basis" in the home; how much you paid originally for tax purposes. The accountant will also ask about any major upgrades performed during your residency. Provide a copy to your accountant and attorney. Here is a starter list of documents for the file.

- Settlement Statement (closing statement)
- Title Insurance Policy
- Mortgage Documents
- Appraisal
- Hazard Insurance Policy
- Home Warranty
- Inspection reports (physical inspections, foundation, pests)
- Information on appliances or upgraded major systems

The Day After Closing

Welcome home! Now change the locks! This is the first thing to do. Granted, utility changeover is a necessity, but safety tops the list so you may want to call a locksmith a few days before closing day to schedule this for the day of closing.

Remarkably, the day after closing most everyone at the table has disappeared (as they are on to the next customer transaction). It's just you, a set of keys (remember to change the locks) and a new life to start as a homeowner. Give yourself some time to settle in. Rome was not built in a day nor is everything going to find a way to where it belongs for a little while.

The best way to move from one home to another is to pack up one room at a time then unpack one room at time at the destination. This seldom happens, though, as things are misplaced and mislabeled. Speed lends itself to accidents, so take your time with those heavy boxes and big pieces of furniture. There is more to moving that just boxes. See After Steps on the next page.

Action Steps After Closing:

- Check that all new keys work in all new locks.
- Test security alarm to make sure it is in working order.
- Review home owners' insurance policy.

Website References:

JohnWilhoit.com – click on Home-Ownership for a free email course "10 Ways to Find Your Down Payment".

Go here to find out more about the home study course based on the book "12 Steps to Home-Ownership".

Visit often for updates and free information about home-ownership, Real Estate Investing and Property Management

After Steps

You- the new homeowner. Wow! Things to do...

Things to do...

A worst-case scenario occurred recently in my home town where a homeowner went on an extended vacation leaving keys with their neighbor and best friend. The neighbor's teenage grandson took the keys and proceeded to throw parties at the house...for days and days. The house was essentially destroyed on the inside. All from one key getting into the wrong hands.

- Change the locks! Yes, you received keys at closing. Now dump them- fast! Here is why: because you don't know who may have a key. Kids, grand kids, neighbors, the prior owners' best friend. An out-of-town friend that they "forgot" to tell they have moved. An ex-husband or wife, current and future convicts! All locks include all doors with locks- every entry door: garage, basement, deck entry- every lock.

- Change your address. Your creditors want to know where you live. So does aunt Mary and that cousin always borrowing tools and raiding the frig.

- Changing over utilities. Since you have completed a thorough review of all the utilities and service providers already. This is a simple step but double-check that all prior utilities are transferred and that all former accounts are closed.

- Garage door openers. These are electronic keys so make sure to reboot and change the codes.

- Insurance- read the binder for exclusions: Every policy has exclusions. For example, most do not cover flood. Some exclude wind and hail.

- Coupons. You will get many for a season. Even though you may not have told a single soul about your new move everybody already knows- at least the retailers know. It is a matter of public record. It's on the county tax roll that a piece of property changed hands. This event was recorded at closing and is now public information.

- When I suggest that everybody knows, I mean EVERYBODY. This includes service providers that will be sending you lots of mail with special offers including but not limited to; interest free furniture purchases, one-time gift cards for towels and sheets for $25, carpet cleaning, window washing, painters and candlestick makers all.

- Consider changing out all existing light bulbs to hi-efficiency bulbs. The easiest way to do this is to just change existing bulbs with new high efficiency bulbs as the old ones go out. It may take some time using this method but you will have removed every old bulb over time.

- If painting, consider replacing all light switch and outlet covers. Here is why: If the paint is "original" then so too are the covers. Putting back the old is like the proverbial saying of putting lipstick on a pig. Plus, new covers are very inexpensive when purchased in contractor's packs of ten per box.

- Review interior light fixtures. Here is why: aside from fresh paint changing antiquated light fixtures can bring a quick newness to a home. Look for places to install a nice ceiling fan or unique lighting ornaments to provide some character.

- Factor in some new furniture. Here's why; because he or she will want some new furniture to go with the new house. Count on it.

- Review locations for flat screen televisions. Here is why: connectivity at the perfect spot cannot be presumed. There may be cause to install new electrical wiring or outlets to gain access to that "perfect spot" in addition to cable. Granted, we are moving into the age of wireless TV but cable hard wiring is still in wide use.

- Landscaping is an asset. Throw some grass seed while thinking about what you might want to do with the yard.

- Clean and test HVAC during good weather. Have Freon levels checked. Change air filters – all.

- Clean gutters or hire someone to clean them.

- House warming party? Make it for a month or so after move-in, during a good weather season.

- Clean chimney and clothes dryer vent all the way to the outside air.

- Address squeaky doors and steps before they become a continuing nuisance.

- Review air ducts. Have them professionally cleaned if necessary. Necessary if a non-smoker is moving in behind a smoker.

- Repair and clean all window screens.

- Check to see if the pet invisible fence is working.

Conclusion

For people that read the conclusion first, the defining the scope of this book is to draw a road map to the decision-making process for becoming a home-owner. Missing a step can at best prolong the process and at worst make for a miserable experience because of unnecessary expenditures caused by a lack of knowledge, guidance, pride or ignorance.

When I read a book, I hope to learn at least one new actionable thing. When I am writing a book, my intention is to bring new knowledge to a wide audience and convey to my audience at least one new point of knowledge from each chapter. Hopefully, I have exceeded that meager goal herein.

More importantly, my hope is this book becomes your reference guide as you walk (and sometimes run) through the home buying experience with just a little less mystery and a lot more facts from day one. Remember to breath!

Are You Ready to Go Further?

Please visit JohnWilhoit.com to find out more about the "12 Steps to Home-Ownership" home study course and online course that will take you even deeper into the home-buying sequence.

Sign up for our newsletter to get timely information and updates about home-ownership, real estate investing and property management. Select "Home-Ownership" on JohnWilhoit.com to get free email courses and webinars. Please read the next few pages to learn more about the online course.

Attention, Soon-To-Be Home-Owners!

Are you Ready to Start the Journey to Home-Ownership?

AN ONLINE COURSE BASED ON THE BOOK "12-STEPS TO HOME-OWNERSHIP"

If you think home-ownership is out of reach, if you think it's too complicated, too expensive and can't happen to you, then you're about to read the letter you've been waiting for all your life. Here's why:

Home-ownership is a process. Gone are the days when "fogging a mirror" can get you a loan. But I'm getting ahead of myself.

The "12 Steps to Home-Ownership" Online Course will help you build your personal road map to home-ownership: from making the home-ownership decision to implementing the sequence for getting it done.

Home-Ownership is Hard, But Not Impossible

How many times have you started on the path to home-ownership only to be thrown off course by mountains of information, a lack of good advice and fast-talking sales people looking to make a quick buck?

Home-ownership is a decision, one that will change your life and your financial future. To get there requires finding the right people to help you arrive with grace and less anxiety while avoiding the grind and grunge caused by fakers and takers of your time, energy and effort.

The impossible becomes possible once you surround yourself with the right team, resources and a process that keeps you on task, on course and focused on the result: home-ownership!

The 12 Steps to Home-Ownership Online Course presents a personal do-it-yourself mandate to getting on track to purchase a home. The course provides tools and guidance for asking the right questions as you make your way through the home-buying decision-making process.

Sequence is the Key to Success

In this online course, as you work through each module you can immediately set about the task of becoming a home-owner with little guess-work. You will be asking the right questions that guide your path to the goal while side-stepping parts and places that get most people confused, off track and unable to recover. While others are stuck with no way out you will keep moving from step to step having reached the goal!

Each module dives deep into the thinking behind the "how" and "why" ending with specific action steps to accomplish one phase of the home-ownership process before moving on to the next. The result is YOU - the home-owner!

- Determine Exactly How Much House You Can Afford
- Finding That Special Place to Call Home
- Choosing Your Own Colors and Carpet
- Parking in Your Very Own Garage

Who is the Instructor and Why Should I Listen to him?

The Instructor is John Wilhoit. John is the author of several books about real estate investing and management include "12 Steps to

Home-Ownership." You can find his books on JohnWilhoit.com and Amazon. In his career as a real estate asset manager, John was responsible for the financial and physical care of real estate assets all over the country valued at more than three-hundred million of dollars. He has owned millions of dollars in real estate assets personally and has purchased many homes personally.

John wrote the book "12 Steps to Home-Ownership" as a gateway for residential home-owners-to-be to streamline the home-ownership process, as a reference guide and road map for people with some or no knowledge of the process- as a way for people to get on track and stay on track until the goal is achieved.

Who should take this course?

Anyone seriously thinking about becoming a home-owner. There are a lot of steps to gaining home-ownership. This course outlines the right steps, 100+ Action steps: these are the "cobblestones" (smaller steps) beneath the 12 Steps- the bedrock for building your plan for getting through the entire process with grace and ease. That may seem like a lot but consider trying this WITHOUT the road map! It's not about the number of steps, frankly, it's about taking the right steps in the right sequence.

- Make the Go-No Go Decision
- Consider Your Exit Strategy- Before You Buy
- Build Your Home Buying Team – You Never Have To Go It Alone
- Decide on Property Type Before Every Seeing a Single Property
- Learn the Action Steps That Count

The 12 Steps to Home-Ownership Online Course, is a practical step-by-step guide about buying your first home while avoiding as many pitfalls as possible.

My objective is to save you hundreds of hours and thousands of dollars in wasted time energy and effort in pursuit of homes that are outside of your sweet spot, personally, financially or geographically. We want you to stay focused on what works for you.

Each module ends with specific "Action Steps" to accomplish before going to the next step in the home-buying process.

12 Steps to Home-ownership is for you if you have a willingness to become educated about the process in advance so that when the opportunity presents itself you are ready!

Course Modules That Take You Step, by Step, by Step

The book "12 Steps to Home-Ownership, presents 36 action steps and multiple website references to get the job done. The 12 Steps to Home-Ownership Online Course goes deeper and presents over 100+ action steps (in sequence) for getting the job done along with 50+ web site references to prepare you for the task of purchasing a home.

- Define Your Neighborhoods of Interest
- Choose the "Where" – In Advance
- Know the Neighborhood Boundaries That Matter
- Find That Perfect Place

Each Module has multiple lectures, hand-outs (downloads) and instructor narrative to give you everything you need to get on the path to home-ownership.

Answering the question of where you want to live creates a queasy feeling for many people; because we know where we "want" to live, then there is where we can afford to live. Balancing these two is discussed in depth as part of the process of buying your first home.

Making a Quality Decision for You and Your Family

This course is designed to prepare you for that moment in time when you can sign a contract for a home with confidence knowing that you've made a quality decision for you and your family.

I believe the content of this course will set you on a path to home-ownership. Home-ownership is the bedrock of building personal wealth. There is no buying a second home, or third, without first buying the first one, right? Of course, there is far more to the process than just picking out a home with pretty colors and a nice door front.

What the Federal Reserve Knows About Home-Ownership

The Federal Reserve is run by the Board of Governors of the Federal Reserve. The Federal Reserve Board of Governors is nominated by the President of the United States and confirmed by the Senate. Their role is to protect and preserve the economy of the country. Once every three years the Federal Reserve completes a survey of consumers that includes information related to homeownership.

The outputs of this survey range in value from one survey to the next, but the bottom line is this; homeowners are found to have a net worth of thirty to fifty times greater than non-homeowners. That's 30 to 50 times greater!!!

- Build Wealth for You and Your Family
- Increase Your Net Worth 30-50 Times Higher Than Renters
- Have a Place to Call Home That Is Yours – not the Landlords!

What Is Our Value Proposition?

I believe each hour you devote to this course will save you ten or more hours in your journey towards becoming a home-owner: one day with the online course "12-Steps to Home-Ownership" could save you ten days! That's ten days you can devote to pursuing a home with the right tools to get it done right!

Even better, and more to the point, this course will save you not just hours, but potentially thousands of dollars in opportunity costs from pursuing the wrong homes in the wrong neighborhoods that should have never made the cut- that is, if you had used the processes in the course to get right to the sweet spot of homes that fit you from the beginning, personally and financially.

- Knowing What You Can Afford before you Start Looking
- Building the right team with the right tools
- Beyond Theory – delivering the right steps- in sequence
- Action Steps that outline what to do next

Our Goal Is to Save You Time, Money and Frustration. Time. Is. Money.

The 12 Steps to Home-Ownership Online Course is a do-it-yourself road map to home-buying providing tools and guidance for asking the right questions in advance of making the home buying decision. It is a guide to assist in your personal journey in the home-buying decision-making process.

For the home-owner-to-be please join me. The time you devote here can save you hundreds of hours and thousands of dollars.

Our Guarantee

What if I am unhappy with the course? We would never want you to be unhappy! If you are unsatisfied with your purchase, contact us in the first 30 days and we will give you a full refund.

Order Now!

Click to Order "12 Steps to Home-Ownership the Online Course." Register to take the course and you will have one full year of access to the course. You can download the extended Action Steps for each chapter immediately.

PS

Purchasing a home is a big decision. You need the right tools at the right time to get it done with grace and less stress. With this online course, with building the right team and focusing your energy in the right places you will have the confidence to know your purchase is one that fits you and your lifestyle in a place of your choosing (not someone else's choosing). Click here to order and streamline your steps to buying the home of your dreams...

Remodeling On A Budget – by John Wilhoit
A New Book for Release in 2018…

INTRODUTION

This book is about home remodeling and renovation; not a single project but remodeling or renovating an entire house. But wait! Isn't remodeling an entire house a collection of individual remodeling projects? Yes! But where to start? What makes sense considering your goals and budget? The "big picture" should encompass your goals and a timeline for completion. And while budget is important, you'll be surprised at the things you can accomplish with limited dollars. Defining the "scope of work" is key.

I had a remodeling project at my house budgeted at $5,000. It came in at $13,000. Is that a problem? Well, yea. What happen? No one was in charge- least of all me. I was "too busy" working.

The good news about remodeling and renovation projects is that they can and should have a start date, an end date and a budget. Paying attention during the process is important. That doesn't mean parking yourself on the floor in front of the project at hand and becoming obnoxious. Being meaningfully engaged also doesn't mean quitting your day job to act as a hall monitor. The devil is in the details. The details are in planning the work- on paper (or in an electronic file) that guides the work towards an on-time and on budget conclusion.

The further out on the calendar your remodel project is the less likely it is to occur. There are many farmyard barns that have fallen back into the earth that someone intended to repair "one day". At some point, it becomes easier to build a new barn than fix the old barn. People do the same thing with houses: they know what is required to bring their current home up to par, but it's just easier to move to another home (or a newly constructed home) where everything is already done.

Yet, there are times when the current home is just irreplaceable to you and your family. It's in the exact right spot on the earth, you have known the neighbors forever and the kids love their school. Why would you ever leave? Well. There's a few things wrong with our "garden spot". The windows let in air, there's a hole in the driveway one foot deep and every year the trees dump one hundred million pounds of leaves by the front door. It's easy to say replace the windows, fill in the hole and remove the trees; easier said than done.

There is a cost associated with each of these and, in many parts of the country, a best season to accomplish the task. Then there is the matter of deciding which one to do first what takes priority and why. And as soon as there is a list...the list gets longer and longer leading to confusion, a sense of being overwhelmed and finally defeat (let's just forget the whole thing).

This book is intended to get you past the confusion, beyond that sinking feeling of "this is too much" and set out a plan for progress to accomplish a remodel you will be proud of while limiting "brain damage" from frustration, costs-overruns and shoddy workmanship.

There are some good books on the market to assist the Do-It-Yourself crowd in lining up the right tools and materials to tackle any remodeling job. This book is for the rest of us; those that have a decent idea about what we want done yet needing skilled labor to get it done. We too want to remodel and do it right the first time.

This book provides a roadmap to that end without having to know a right angle from a radiating heat pump.

This book does not assume that you personally have any "fix-it" skills whatsoever (present company included). Nor will I suggest relying on friends, neighbors or the kindness of strangers. We all make choices. The decision to remodel or renovate your home can be a major financial decision. But it doesn't have to be. Some of the most beneficial and personally satisfying remodeling projects are small and quaint yet impactful in terms of their personal enjoyment to you, the homeowner.

First and foremost, safety is the number one task. There is nothing more important than starting and finishing a remodeling project without injury to any person. That is part of what makes remodeling such a chore; understanding the level of hazard to life and limb. Most people know that shooting electricity through their body is a bad thing. If you are unfamiliar with the term bearing wall (a wall that bears the weight of the house above) then it's a safe to say you should not be the one knocking down walls. Any remodel job, large or small, do-it-yourself or hired out, should have safety as priority.

Please be sure to read the interviews with long-time professionals. They are insightful and will yield you huge benefits and time-saving tips.

Index

A

Acceptance 91, 102
Advisors 8, 75, 76, 77, 85, 89, 103
Affordability 2, 8, 9, 49, 74
Apartment i, 28, 29
Appraisal 114
Appreciation 17

B

Bank statements 113
Budget xi, 131

C

Census 35, 36, 40, 42
Closing 111, 114, 115, 116
Condo 24, 28, 30, 89, 90, 93
Condominium 28

D

Demographic ii, 34, 35, 39, 40, 41, 42, 48
Demographics 33, 34
Depreciation 17
Door 108

E

Economy 12, 127
Exit Strategy 15, 84, 125

F

Fixed Rate Mortgage 82
Fixer's 93, 94
Fixer-upper's 94
Flooring 26, 94
Foreclosure 95
For Sale by Owner 93
FSBO 93, 94

H

Home Equity 83
Home Inspection 68, 105, 107, 110
Homeowners Associations 30
Home Ownership xv, 9, 17, 39, 66
House Hunting 87

I

Inspection xvii, 95, 96, 113, 114

K

Kitchen 10, 55, 93

L

Lender 66, 67, 68, 69, 70, 74, 75, 76, 82, 83, 85, 89, 94, 95, 102, 107, 112, 113, 114

M

Mortgage i, 4, 5, 6, 10, 11, 12, 13, 17, 18, 29, 49, 69, 70, 74, 75, 76, 77, 82, 83, 85, 94, 95, 109, 113, 114

N

Neighborhoods 39, 92, 126

P

Paint 94, 108
Paperwork 69, 76, 113
Pest 107, 110
Pets 59
Pre-approved 85, 89

R

Real Estate Owned 95
Realtor 67, 103
Rent 2, 5, 10, 14, 17, 29, 30
REO 93, 95

S

Single-Family 27
Submarkets 48

T

Term of Residency 19
Title 70, 114
Townhome 89

U

Utilities 107

V

Variable Rate Mortgage 18, 82

W

Warranty 114
Website References 32, 42, 51, 63, 71, 85, 98, 103, 110, 116

www.ingramcontent.com/pod-product-compliance
Lightning Source LLC
Chambersburg PA
CBHW060035210326
41520CB00009B/1140